Hockey

Dr. Randy Gregg

Hockey

The Technical, The Physical, and The Mental Game

Hockey: The Technical, the Physical, and the Mental Game
by Dr. Randy Gregg
ISBN: 0-9682970-7-2

FP Hendriks Publishing Ltd.
4806–53 St.
Stettler, AB T0C 2L2
Fax/Phone: (403) 742-6483
Toll Free Fax/Phone: 1-888-374-8787
E-mail: editor@fphendriks.com
Website: www.fphendriks.com

Canadian Cataloguing in Publication Data
Gregg, Randy, 1956–
    Hockey

(LifeSport books)
ISBN 0-9682970-3-X

    1. Hockey—Coaching. 2. Hockey—Training. I. Title. II. Series
GV848.25.G73 1999   796.962′07′7   C99-911111-6

Production Team
Thanks to all those talented people who worked on this project:

Author	Dr. Randy Gregg
Project Director	Faye Boer
Illustrator	Ross Palsson
Cover Design	Brad Fischer, Speedfast Color Press Inc.
Page Layout & Design	Kerry Plumley
Editors	Faye Boer; Barb Demers
Photos	Hank Boer; Brian Gavriloff, The Edmonton Journal
Validators	Clare Drake; Dr. Betty Ross; Connie Walker-Dymianiw

Manufacturers
Transcontinental Press; Speedfast Color Press Inc.
PRINTED IN CANADA

Dedication

To my sister, Judy, whose courage, spirit,
compassion, and determination will forever
keep me focused on my lifelong goals.

Hockey

The Technical, The Physical, and The Mental Game

Acknowledgements

I would like to thank the validators who assisted with this book.

Clare Drake has been a fantastic role model for thousands of young men and women who have crossed his path both on the hockey ice and off. Without his leadership and influence, my career and that of others like me would never have blossomed as they did. Because of his wisdom, commitment, and high moral standard, I will always welcome any suggestions or information from Clare Drake. I continue to feel privileged to know him as a friend.

I first met Betty Ross when she was the team physician with Canada's Olympic Hockey team in 1988. While enjoying her wit, genuine interest in people, and her penchant for practical jokes, I also discovered a competent sport medicine physician who was committed, first and foremost, to the ultimate welfare of the athlete. I have tried to follow her lead by always keeping in mind that the most important person in sport is not the coach, parent, or doctor, but rather the player! I appreciate Betty's time in validating the medical information included in this book.

Validators

Clare Drake, former coach, University of Alberta Golden Bears Hockey

Dr. Betty Ross, BPT, MD, CCFP, Diploma in Sports Medicine, Certified Independent Medical Examiner

Connie Walker-Dymianiw, Kevin Sirois Fitness Center, Red Deer College (Stretches in Chapter 5)

Cover Photos

Front Cover: Thanks also to those enthusiastic players who allowed their photos to appear on the cover. They are Zachary Bowles, Charlee Mappin, and Peter Boer.

Back Cover: Randy and Kathy Gregg with their children, Jamie, Ryan, Jessica, and Sarah

Foreword

The game of hockey, as most Canadians know, is an important and complex component of our culture. It has a uniqueness to it and has the ability to shake us with its confusing patterns of success and failure. It also leads us to some remarkable self-discoveries, both of our capabilities and of our limitations.

For those people—parents, coaches, and hockey association administrators—who want to provide the best possible environment for the young athletes in their charge, this book provides unique insights into aspects of hockey that previously have not often been adequately addressed.

The physical and behavioral learning environment that we create for our young hockey players has a dramatic effect on their opportunity for personal development from both a physical skills and a socialization standpoint. Randy has done an excellent job of outlining a series of progression drills that lead us through the important basic hockey skills.

The sections on injury identification and on-ice and off-ice training come with great credibility given his extensive medical and rehabilitative background to go along with his quality playing experiences in both intercollegiate and professional hockey.

One of the goals that everyone involved in amateur hockey has to be conscious of is maintaining the elements of fun and enjoyment. This book faithfully reminds us of the importance of maintaining an enjoyable environment for the participants.

Parents, coaches, and sports association administrators have an obligation to use their influence in a positive, ethical manner. I believe that this book provides the type of information that will help guide them in the right direction. I have a great respect for Randy Gregg and his views, and congratulate him for sharing his knowledge and experiences with the people who will read this book.

Clare Drake,
former coach of the University of Alberta
Golden Bears Hockey Team

Randy Gregg, 1983

HOCKEY

1 - Introduction

We often expect new coaches to fully understand game strategy, give accurate nutritional advice, teach precise technical skills, run a well-organized practice, and know how to handle a severe on-ice injury. With such high expectations, it is a wonder that we have *any* first-year coaches who volunteer! It is a tribute to volunteerism and to the great game of hockey that every year each hockey team has an enthusiastic coach who is willing to lead each team into competition. While expectations for coaches can seem unrealistic, I hope to provide some tips and "inside information" that will help hockey coaches everywhere cope with the demands of the game, the players, and the public!

In Canada, the National Coaching Certification Program and in the US, USA Hockey Inc. have developed comprehensive sets of coaching certification levels so that coaches can expand their knowledge of the game. Many coaches have progressed through the Initiation, Coach, Intermediate, and Advanced levels in their pursuit of a better understanding of this fine game. My purpose in writing this book is to help bridge the gap between

understanding and application of learned skills for minor hockey coaches as they continue to refine their coaching skills within the Certification Program.

This book is also for parents who wish to both help their children achieve their potential while helping them keep the game in perspective. *Hockey: The Technical, the Physical, and the Mental Game* provides coaches and parents with an easy-to-use reference on a wide variety of important hockey topics. Written in three distinct sections, this book identifies three basic components of hockey development—the technical, the physical, and the mental.

Three Components of Hockey Development
1. *Technical*
2. *Physical*
3. *Mental*

The Technical component of the book describes the ten important on-ice skills that are essential for optimal hockey performance: speed, agility, power, puckhandling, passing, checking, positional play, intuition, and work ethic. I have also included my drill favorites for each of the ten skills. The Technical section will be especially useful for coaches who wish to incorporate a more complete goalie development component into their practice organization. I have described goalie skills in detail and included some of my drill favorites to help these important players improve their skills.

The Physical component of the book discusses the importance of developing an all-round athlete. Enhanced athleticism is a valuable first step in becoming a strong, well-rounded hockey player. Very often skilled, strong hockey players are also proficient in other sports. Proper eating habits, warmups, and conditioning enhance on-ice performance while developing lifelong healthy habits, especially if coaches and parents promote these early in a young skater's career. These routines may someday make the difference between being on a championship team or watching helplessly from the stands with an injury!

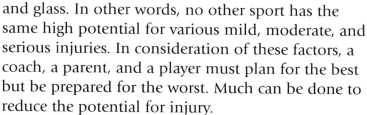

No sport compares to hockey's speed, finesse, and physical contact. It is a sport that demands twelve players wearing razor-sharp, unprotected skate blades to challenge each other for control of a small rubber disk on an ice surface surrounded by rigid boards and glass. In other words, no other sport has the same high potential for various mild, moderate, and serious injuries. In consideration of these factors, a coach, a parent, and a player must plan for the best but be prepared for the worst. Much can be done to reduce the potential for injury.

Protective equipment has become a great deal more sophisticated over the years, while still allowing for the smooth flow of puck and player. The Equipment chapter will help beginning coaches and new hockey parents make informed decisions when purchasing, using, and maintaining hockey equipment.

The Injury chapter is an excellent reference for coaches and parents to help prevent injuries or to expedite responsible treatment once an injury has

THE TECHNICAL, THE PHYSICAL, AND THE MENTAL GAME

occurred. While not intended to replace the need for professional medical care, ***Hockey: The Technical, the Physical, and the Mental Game*** provides some helpful hints regarding identification, treatment, and rehabilitation of common hockey injuries. Each area of the body (starting with the head and ending at the feet) is discussed in detail. How an injured limb might look or how a player might feel, as well as how to identify common hockey injuries, will help coaches make an important assessment before returning an injured player to the line-up. This chapter also includes important information on how to develop an Emergency Action Plan. Every hockey team must have a well-practiced Emergency Action Plan in place so that, in the event of a serious injury, proper and timely measures can be taken to reduce the risk of further injury and to determine whether professional medical attention is required.

> *Every hockey team must have a well-practiced Emergency Action Plan in place...*

The Fitness Training chapter of this book outlines the importance of adding a dryland-training component to regular on-ice practice sessions and provides examples of fitness-enhancing drills for both on and off the ice. A regular training program in a gym or a community hall contributes to the making of better hockey players and better athletes. This can be accomplished in an enjoyable yet challenging fashion and at a cost far less than more ice time. As the 1980s and 1990s brought in an acceptance of mandatory helmets, the new millennium will also herald the arrival of physical training as an integral part of hockey development.

The final section looks at the Mental component of hockey. I found this the most enjoyable part of the book to write as it brought back memories of my coach Father David Bauer, the man for whom I have the utmost respect. He was the ultimate sportsman—intensely competitive and always trying to get the most from each of his players. Unlike many other coaches, though, he did not allow his competitive spirit to lead him astray from his primary goal in sport—the development of the whole person through athletics. If he were alive today, Father Bauer would like the title, *Hockey: The Technical, the Physical, and the Mental Game*, because he believed that hockey was too fine a game to play simply to see who wins.

I have had the privilege to play under some amazing coaches over the years—Clare Drake was a masterful teacher on the ice and a fine gentleman and role model off the ice; John Muckler was the tactician who analyzed opposition strengths and developed successful strategies for playing against them; and, of course, Father Bauer had the relentless goal of making hockey a true learning experience for all who participated. The chapter entitled "Attitudes in Hockey" will ring true for many hockey coaches who persevere in the face of personality conflicts and verbally abusive parents in an environment where too many focus solely on winning rather than on learning. In this chapter, I offer a coaching philosophy compiled from observations of many of the great coaches for whom I had the privilege of playing.

Finally and possibly most important, this section includes information on how hockey players can prepare mentally for the game. After playing fifteen years in minor hockey, four years with the University of Alberta Golden Bears, two Olympic Games, nine years in the National Hockey League including five Stanley Cup championships and one Canada Cup championship, I have seen many instances where mental strength and preparation have made the difference between good players and truly great ones. There are hundreds of thousands of good hockey players in the world today but only a few who dare to become great. Mental training and preparation can make the difference!

I have been involved with the sport of hockey for thirty-five years. I now coach my own sons in the game that has given me so much. As well, I have watched with joy the expansion of female hockey and their ability to display speed, finesse, and determination on the Olympic and World stages. With a young daughter presently enjoying her hockey experience, I am confident that the information in this book will be equally valuable and applicable to male and female coaches and players alike.

Please enjoy the book as you use it during your hockey seasons. I hope that the game of hockey is as fulfilling and enjoyable for you and your players as it has been for me.

Yours in sporting,

Randy

The Technical Game

individual skills, goalie skills

THE TECHNICAL GAME

T here are three components of preparation—technical, physical, mental—that are important to becoming a successful hockey player. Of the three, the technical component is the most obvious. Although many coaches have different styles of coaching and varying philosophies towards skill development, most agree that there are basically ten individual hockey skills required by players in order to be successful. These skills include skating speed, agility, power, puckhandling, passing, shooting, checking, positional play, intuition, and work ethic. Each of these individual skills is fully described with accompanying drills in Chapter 2, "Individual Skills."

It is widely thought that development of individual skills should be the basis for early levels of minor hockey organizations. Young players, ages four to ten, require repetitive practice in each of these skill areas in order to become proficient players. Strong minor hockey organizations focus youth programs strictly on the improvement of individual skills, so that a strong foundation is set for further development as the players mature both physically and mentally. Of course, once a player reaches the age of fourteen or fifteen, individual skills should not be forgotten, but can usually be

Father David Bauer once revealed his discussions with senior Russian hockey administrators back in the 1960s. The Russians, not yet acknowledged as a world power in hockey by most North Americans, explained that they believed hockey could be broken down into five one-on-ones any time during a game. Their view was that the team who won the majority of the one-on-one battles would eventually be the victors. As a result, they spent considerable time and energy developing these individual skills. It is interesting to see the results of this view today. Russian players currently on National Hockey League teams are some of the most highly skilled players in the league. Is this a trend that minor hockey organizations can learn—spending considerable energy on skillful coaching with an emphasis on individual hockey skills?

practiced as an integrated component of team-oriented drills.

Chapter 3, "Goalie Skills," is included to help coaches instruct and provide direction for the players who are sometimes left to their own devices—the goaltenders. Coaches may be able to teach skills to forwards and defensemen, but sometimes do not have a wide range of drills for the goaltender. It is true that many of the skills required by the goaltender—skating, agility, puckhandling, and passing—are the same as for any player although a goalie may use these skills in different ways. There are also skills that are unique to this position—positional awareness, up and down skills, crease movement, glove skills, and rebound control. It is important that these young players have the chance to develop their skills in the same way as the rest of the team. Chapter 3 provides coaches with an understanding of the skills required by goalies as well as drills to improve these skills.

Both chapters in this section provide support for coaches in teaching skills. The Appendix also provides sample practice plans to organize both on-ice and dryland practices for working on specific skill areas and blank templates for adapting the plan to a coach's personal style. It is my hope that if coaches emphasize the skills outlined in these two chapters as early as possible, then young players will benefit by becoming the best players they can be.

> *"The difference between a successful person and others is not a lack of strength nor a lack of knowledge, but rather a lack of will."*
> *–Vince Lombardi*

2 - Individual Skills

Because it is a game of high speed, physical contact, and fast-paced action, hockey demands many specialized skills from its participants. One of the main responsibilities of a coach is to help players develop these skills through good practice organization, assessment, and positive feedback. Before plunging into teaching specific hockey skills, however, it is important to gain a perspective on skill development. There are two ways to do this:

1. *Separate the game into its basic components.*
2. *Teach skills progressively.*

School teachers know the most effective ways to teach children valuable educational information. The wide scope of information that children must learn in school includes reading and writing skills, mathematics, science, and social studies. These academic subjects (or information groups) have been artificially separated to make it easier for a student to learn and understand information. Too much information overwhelms rather than informs. Can you imagine a teacher in the middle of a science lesson abruptly switching gears and giving out a math assignment? Only when a student becomes more experienced and mature is it appropriate to combine all the educational components, forming a mosaic of overall learning. Sounds a little bit like coaching hockey!

> *Breaking information into smaller components makes it easier for students to learn.*

Most hockey experts agree that there are several specific individual hockey skills that players must learn before their "hockey mosaic" becomes fundamentally strong. I have identified ten skills that encompass the most important aspects of a young hockey player's development.

1. Speed
2. Agility
3. Power
4. Puckhandling
5. Passing
6. Shooting
7. Checking
8. Positional Play
9. Intuition
10. Work Ethic

A Perspective on Skill Development

Before teaching skills in isolation, however, it is important to place the teaching of those skills into an overall perspective. Any experienced hockey person can teach the skills listed; however, it is often the *way* these skills are taught that makes the difference between success on the ice and a frustrated group of players who have the skills but have an incomplete understanding of how to apply them in a game situation. Players gain an understanding of the way the game works and can apply specific skills when coaches

> 1. *teach the basic components of the game and*
> 2. *teach skills progressively.*

TEACH THE BASIC COMPONENTS OF THE GAME

It is important for coaches to divide the sometimes-confusing game of hockey into its specific components, especially for young players. For example, most players would probably say that they prefer to scrimmage for the whole practice. They consider it to be the most fun. However, playing a game or scrimmaging involves the integration of many skills. For a developing player, a scrimmage is a difficult environment for learning and one in which poor habits are easily acquired. With so many actions and developing plays all over the ice during a scrimmage, it is more difficult to single out specifics for learning purposes. By separating the many skills required in a scrimmage into individual components that can more easily be practiced in isolation, coaches can foster good habits and slowly build on what players have learned so that the game becomes a more dynamic challenge for players.

...separate the many skills required in a scrimmage into individual components that can more easily be practiced in isolation...

Even experienced players benefit from practices where the focus is on isolated skills such as speed, agility, or the power components of skating. As the players' skills become more developed, coaches can slowly integrate two skills into a particular practice drill, then three, and so on. Soon players are able to practice more complex drills that closely simulate game situations. More important though, players develop improved hockey skills and are less likely to acquire bad habits or miss the essential elements that make up a well-rounded hockey player.

TEACH SKILLS PROGRESSIVELY

Keep in mind the teaching strategies that are used each weekday in school classrooms everywhere. The curriculum outlines levels of learning, concepts, and skills that are appropriate for the children of a certain age or grade in specific subjects such as math, science, language arts, or physical education. Teachers then write year plans, unit plans, and daily lesson plans to teach students these skills and concepts. Once the desired level of learning is attained, teachers then reset their teaching goals to a higher level and begin to further stimulate the students into expanding their knowledge base. Called progressive learning, this highly developed process begins in kindergarten and continues through elementary, junior high, high school, and on into post-secondary learning.

Progressive learning can also be used successfully by coaches. More importantly, minor hockey organizations with a vision for the future could encourage the use of a progressive learning system that uses a consistent approach to skill development throughout the season and from one season to the next. Valuable learning opportunities and highly developed skills are enhanced in minor hockey when established and progressive drill and practice patterns are used consistently by all coaches. Having each coach trying to teach hockey drills in a unique way does not accomplish nearly as much. A consistent approach eliminates the need for players to learn and to adapt to an all-new set of drills, terms, and practice dynamics at the beginning of each season.

Of course, players benefit from exposure to a variety of coaching styles. Every player is likely to be taught by quiet, reserved coaches, more aggressive, motivating individuals, as well as by coaches who love to yell and scream. As a result of this varied exposure, athletes form attitudes about how different coaching styles affect them. They will develop their own sense of coaching tactics and attitudes that they will eventually use when they become team leaders. While exposure

Playing with the University of Alberta Golden Bears hockey team was a fantastic experience. Not only did I have the opportunity to combine high level athletics with post-secondary academics; I was also exposed to a successful program where the fundamental goal of skill development revolved around consistent and progressive learning. As a rookie everything was new and practice time was a great challenge both physically and mentally. By the second year I began to understand practice procedure where vital individual and team drills were repeated consistently throughout the season to emphasize their importance for ultimate success. In the third year I made great advances in skill development during practice because I was so familiar with the drills. I spent much more time on execution and refinement than I did focusing on details of how to perform particular drills. My fourth and last year was a dream. Because of the experience with a consistent, progressively challenging practice program, I became a leader for the rookies, just as the veterans had done for me when I joined the team.

to various coaching techniques and philosophies can be worthwhile, unfortunately it often brings with it a yearly change in fundamental skill teaching and practice organization. It is a huge and daunting task to ask hockey coaches to agree to replace their personal drills and practice organization with a consistent across-the-board organizational approach. However, for the ultimate benefit of young players in that organization, it is well worth the effort!

Consider the difference in outcome for an eight-year-old novice entering a minor hockey program committed to a consistent skill and practice development program. After eight years, this young athlete will have had the benefit of an amazing learning experience, all because of a commitment to excellence at the organizational level!

TEN KEY SKILLS

Many hockey people believe that there are ten key skills that measure a player's ultimate hockey ability. This section will define each skill and show how improvement can occur with a progressive learning program. Each skill is accompanied by the description of one of my drill favorites with at least one option to add to the challenge of the drill. Coaches may wish to adapt these drills to better suit their own practice flow.

> *...there are ten key skills that measure a player's ultimate hockey ability.*

I have collected these drills from coaches at all hockey levels and backgrounds so they are tried and true methods of teaching skills to players. Keep in mind that these few drills are just a sample of a complete set of drills and practice ideas included in *Hockey Drill Solutions*, another book in the *LifeSport* series.

Speed

Definition—the skill that allows a player to get from one place on the ice to another in the shortest possible time

Many times during a game there is a race for a loose puck—a one-on-one battle that ultimately determines which team gets a chance to score. If all other skills are equal, then the faster player always ends up with the puck. In fact, during the 1980s in the NHL it was interesting to see the emphasis shift from size and strength to speed and finesse. The Montreal Canadiens, New York Islanders, and finally the Edmonton Oilers showed the rest of the league that physical presence and size was no match for skating speed and finesse in a duel for puck possession. This trend is continuing with the steady influx of talented European players and, as a result, improved speed continues to give players of all ages a distinct advantage.

KEYS TO EFFECTIVE SPEED DRILLS

First and foremost, there are certain things that a coach should not do during practice. If you asked any hockey player, they would likely say that at one time or another each has heard a coach say, "Okay guys, go hard around the ice five times." The coach is trying to encourage the players to develop their skating speed by including this drill at practice. Unfortunately, it is virtually impossible to skate around the perimeter of the rink five times at absolute top speed.

Players generally skate at 70 to 80% of their top speed, trying to stay with the group of players near them. Because they do not know what to expect for the rest of practice, players generally attempt to save a little energy just in case the coach has planned a late practice conditioning skate. By using such a drill, the coach has inadvertently asked the players to perform at suboptimal speeds, thereby conditioning them both physically and mentally to perform at 80% of maximal effort. An innovative coach, on the other hand, might ask the players to go only three-quarter-speed five times around the ice. The players give the same effort as before, but they and the coach recognize that this is not a speed drill but rather a conditioning and skating technique drill. If a coach wishes to work on skating speed in a practice, then it is essential to use a drill that is truly developed to optimize the players' speed capacity!

> *Players generally skate at 70 to 80% of their top speed… to save a little energy just in case the coach has planned a late practice conditioning skate.*

After many years of watching coaching at every level of hockey, I have gained a great appreciation for the diverse approaches that various coaches take in leading their teams. I have been exposed to coaches who run efficient 60-minute practices as well as those who would carry on for hours and hours if only they had the ice time. Based on these observations and my experience with both amateur and professional coaches, I conclude that, "More is not better." Although in two hours a coach may be able to cover a greater number of drills and repetition in practice, the cost may be high—and not just ice rental cost! Practicing at less than full intensity when the aim is to increase speed reinforces bad habits and ultimately leads to poorer performance. If, as some believe, skating speed is one of the most important skills for hockey players, coaches must then ensure that the appropriate practice drills for speed skating are performed at as high a tempo as possible.

> *Practicing at less than full intensity when the aim is to increase speed reinforces bad habits and ultimately leads to poorer performance.*

Hockey players know that they tend to pace themselves during a practice. Consciously or not, they pace themselves so that they have energy left for the final drills or scrimmage. A two-hour practice virtually guarantees that players execute drills at a slower pace than during two one-hour sessions. If coaches are realistic, then can they say that a slower pace is what they truly want?

What is the solution? It seems obvious that, because ice time is paid by the hour, it is more efficient to schedule two one-hour practices. The cost is the same as one marathon two-hour session and it is possible for players to work harder for the shorter period of time and, as a result, coaches can work their players progressively harder. Clare Drake of the University of Alberta, the greatest coach I had in my hockey career, always scheduled practices that lasted 60 to 75 minutes. Because of his efficiency and great organization, the players got more out of those practices than from many practices twice as long!

An exception to this guideline is the 90-minute practice that is divided into a 60-minute practice session, followed by a short break, and then a 30-minute controlled scrimmage. The coach fulfills practice requirements and still allows players to apply the skills they worked on in practice to a game environment that invariably is played at almost full intensity.

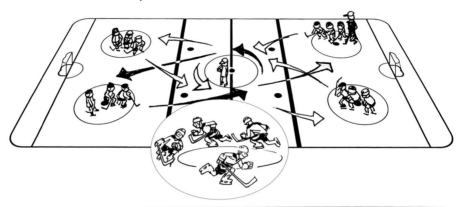

DRILL FAVORITE FOR SPEED

Four Corner Circle Relay

This drill is designed to have players perform at top speed in a competitive challenging environment that pushes them to skate at full intensity.

Objectives

- to develop maximal speed
- to use quick crossovers
- to build team skills
- to have fun at high tempo

Key Teaching Points

- Encourage explosive skating strides.
- Keep head up and knees bent.
- Encourage lots of fun and camaraderie.

Description

Divide players into four equal teams. Each team lines up in one of the corner circles facing the center line. On the whistle, the players at the front of each line skate as fast as possible to the center circle. All skate around the center circle in the same direction then return as fast as possible to their teams. The next player in each line may not leave the team circle until the player ahead reenters the circle. The relay continues until all players have taken a turn. Players go down on one knee after completing the skate, to show the number of remaining players and to rest so that they are fully recovered and able to skate at maximum intensity in the next race.

Drill Options

1. The drill can be performed in both clockwise and counterclockwise directions, forward or backward. Players must perform each variation at full intensity.

2. To add a power component to this drill, one player pushes another player, who is just gliding, around the ice. The pushed player then becomes the pusher and a similar rotation takes place with the remaining team members.

Agility

Definition—the skill that allows a player to change direction quickly and under full control

In the 1970s, teams like the Broad Street Bullies in Philadelphia and the Boston Bruins played hockey in its most simplified form—dump the puck into the zone, chase it, win the battles in the corners and in front of the net, have wingers skate up and down their wings and score more than the other team. During the 1980s, however, the New York Islanders

continued the tradition of toughness but also incorporated an effective offensive component in their game. With players like Mike Bossy and Bryan Trottier, the Islanders had the talent to break from the tradition of "dump and chase" hockey. Skating speed, offensive forechecking, and puck control took on greater importance for this soon-to-be Islander dynasty. Their Stanley Cup successors, the Edmonton Oilers, took the offensive style of play one huge step forward with their flamboyant and talented lineup of stars that included Wayne Gretzky, Mark Messier, Glenn Anderson, and Paul Coffey. With the Oilers' success in the Stanley Cup, hockey gradually became a game of finesse, teamwork, speed, puck control, and agility.

KEYS TO EFFECTIVE AGILITY DRILLS

The ability to change direction quickly is based primarily on two fundamental skills—balance and coordination. It is common to see players who

Wayne Gretzky epitomized the ultimate hockey player during this transition from strength, power, and intimidation to speed, finesse, and puck control. Many marveled at how such a seemingly small player would rarely be caught in a situation where he was hit hard. Some often said that he must have had eyes in the back of his head or that he had incredibly uncanny on-ice anticipation. As a player who had to try to stop him in practice, I realized that one of his most valuable skills was his amazing agility. Trying to contain Wayne was a difficult job, but with his uncanny ability to "thread a needle" with his passing, the Oilers' defensemen were often humbled by his talent that thankfully was on our side during games!

are fast while skating straight but who struggle when they must maneuver with the puck or turn quickly.

Generally this is because these players have not mastered the ability to control their balance on both edges of their skates.

Skaters use the inside edge of a skate during leg push-off. Balance on the inside edge is generally developed early when learning to skate. Balance on the outer edge, however, is not as easy because it requires the confidence to be able to balance body weight much farther away from the center of gravity. Drills designed to make players more comfortable on the outside edge of their skates enhance their skating ability, especially since pushing off the outer skate edge is the first component of a crossover turn or quick pivot.

My wife, Kathy, coaches speed skating following her own career in the sport that took her to two Olympic Games. Although power is a primary component of training in her sport, agility is also important to maximize efficiency in the turns and crossovers. I am always encouraged to see how she uses enjoyable, stimulating drills to enhance skaters' agility, yet she also provides a fun atmosphere. The skaters work at their maximum output with big smiles on their faces. In addition, their parents are happy because the young athletes develop so quickly. Fortunately, Kathy had the opportunity to work with some great coaches during her years on the National Speed Skating Team. Their legacy continues through Kathy because she is passing on not only what she learned but is also promoting speed skating as competitive **and** fun!

Some players think that agility skating drills are boring and not worthy of their full effort. This need not be the case. Creative coaches can incorporate enjoyable agility drills that players will look forward to and consequently will perform at a higher tempo. In fact, most power skating instructors spend more time on agility drills than on power development because agility is the skill that allows youngsters to become proficient skaters much more quickly.

Although there are drills that work specifically on agility, it is a skill that can be incorporated into the vast majority of practice drills. A shooting drill or a checking drill can be modified to include an element of agility. The "Four Corner Circle Relay" (page 22) or the "Breakaway Race" (described on page 45) can be modified for agility training by having the players start on one knee, on their stomachs, or flat on their backs in order to work on body movement, coordination, and balance. Not only do small variations such as these enhance the drills by incorporating a variety of skills, the drills become more fun and more challenging for the players!

From ages twelve to sixteen, youngsters tend to go through a significant growth phase. Because of the rapid physical changes, coordination and balance often deteriorate. These can be difficult times for players because, while their increasing physical size becomes an advantage, it is much harder and more awkward to use it. Effective use of on-ice and off-ice drills during this awkward time with a focus on improving agility allows growing players to make the physical transition with a minimum of difficulty.

DRILL FAVORITE FOR AGILITY

Shadow Drill

In this drill players get used to making quick, agile turns with speed and in traffic.

Objectives

- to develop quick turns
- to improve agility

Key Teaching Points

- Keep head up, especially in tight areas on the ice.
- Anticipate player movement.
- Encourage players to always skate to open areas.

Description

Pair players with others of similar size and skating ability. One player is the leader; the other is the shadow. During the drill players must always skate between the blue lines. On the coach's whistle the leader tries to lose the shadow by skating quickly and by using tight turns. After only eight to ten seconds, the coach blows the whistle again and the players stop and rest. The pairs then switch roles and, after sufficient rest, repeat the drill. During the "Shadow Drill" the players have lots of fun and increase proficiency at skating through traffic.

Drill Options

1. Have players perform this drill between the blue lines so that everyone has room to skate. Once the players are used to the concept of tight space agility, reduce the area to between the blue line and the center line or even inside the center circle.

2. Add pucks for each player during the drill. Players must be comfortable with the skating component before progressing to puckhandling.

Power

Definition—the skill that adds both strength and speed to movement

Hockey commentators often describe a team's "power forward." This is generally a winger, who is not only big and strong but is also able to control both the corners as well as the area in front of the net. This kind of player is valuable to any team, even to those young teams playing in noncontact divisions. The ability to drive hard to the net while fighting off a checker or to go into the corner with an opposing player and come out with the puck are skills that require power. Still, while the fundamental skills required to develop power

(strength and speed) are valuable, they should not be developed in isolation from one another. A speedy hockey player who is easily pushed off the puck is not a great asset to the team. In the same vein, a muscle-bound athlete who cannot skate fast enough to use his strength effectively is similarly handicapped. The combination of speed and strength produces a powerful hockey player, and so drills that enhance power should be included in every practice.

KEYS TO EFFECTIVE POWER DRILLS

Increasing the strength of a particular muscle is achieved by stressing it against resistance, whether it is the quadriceps muscle of the leg that is used during an exploding stride or the biceps muscle in the arm that is used during a slap shot. The principle of overload resistance is used by weight-lifters in every fitness club. To increase strength, it is necessary to push, pull, or lift objects that are of higher resistance or weight than the muscles are presently accustomed to. When apply-ing this principle to hockey, developing a powerful stride means that players must skate as fast as they can against increased resistance.

It is not appropriate or convenient to bring heavy weights onto the ice for power training; in fact, it could be dangerous! In the past instructors have used bungee cords, parachutes, and various other devices to add resistance training to drills, many of which can be effective. Often overlooked, however, is the fact that other players offer the best possible resistance when power training. By pairing players, coaches can develop many on-ice power enhancement drills that incorporate pulling or pushing movements to improve lower and upper body strength. If these resistance drills are done at full speed, then they can also enhance the development of a powerful stride.

Almost every year at training camp in the National Hockey League there is a young player at the first day of tryouts full of confidence with muscles bulging. He is generally a minor league player who did not quite have the skills to make it to the NHL, but with an exceptional training camp may have a chance to play in the "Big Show." He thinks that being stronger might make the difference. The player likely spent all summer lifting weights and doing low repetitions with heavy resistance, trying to bulk up. At training camp this player skates much slower than the other rookies and invariably is sent back to the minors or cut outright. Unfortunately, the player made a fundamental error: strength is not effective unless it is coupled with speed. Each time I saw this happen I felt sorry for the player because it was a simple training error that may have taken away his dream of playing in the National Hockey League.

Coaches must ensure that two components of these drills are fulfilled:

The primary role of John Muckler, assistant coach of the Edmonton Oilers during our Stanley Cup years, was to run practices and to prepare strategy and tactics for upcoming games. He ran a good practice, but one tactic in particular impressed me. It was not unusual for him to include a drill that he called a shooting drill: players would skate the full length of the ice at top speed and end with a shot on goal. He wanted us to begin the drill quickly at top speed and continue to skate hard directly to the front of the net, effectively working on the power component of our skating. The players loved the drill because, of course, we all enjoyed the chance to work on our shooting prowess. However, one day as I was standing in line waiting my turn, I realized that this was more of a power skating drill than a shooting drill, but John had sold it to us as a shooting drill. He got what he wanted, a high tempo skating drill, while we thought we were getting a fun shooting drill. A shrewd coach can motivate players to perform at levels higher than usual simply by selecting good drills and packaging them in an effective practice plan.

1. Players must perform drills at maximum effort. If players skate at half speed, then the training effect is greatly minimized. To ensure players perform at optimum levels, ample rest must be allowed between drill segments so that the players' muscles are ready to perform at maximum effort again. It is not advisable to mix aerobic conditioning with power development in the same drill since these can counteract each other with less than optimal results. The slower paced, longer duration conditioning drills develop stronger heart and lungs but do little to directly improve speed and strength.

2. Make the drills fun. Power drills are hard on players because they require the expenditure of a great deal of energy. Consequently players, especially younger ones, tend to give up easily. Coaches can make power drills fun by adding elements of competition or team building so that the players are motivated to work harder than they might have normally.

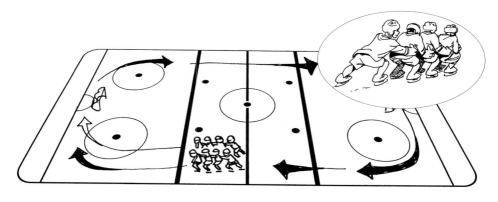

DRILL FAVORITE FOR POWER

Caboose Race

   Players develop powerful strides in a fun and competitive environment.

Objective

• to develop powerful strides

Key Teaching Points

• Work together as a team during transitions.
• Bend knees with full extension during strides.
• Give maximum skating effort.

Description

   Divide players into teams of four. Players lay all sticks on the benches or at the edge of the ice. Line up the players on each team one behind the other, forming a train configuration beginning on one side of the center line. On the whistle each team races in the same direction around goal nets that are pulled in toward center slightly to allow for more room at the ends of the rink. During the drill only the last skater is actually skating. This player pushes the front three, who glide in a bent knee position and hold onto the player in front by the hips. The front player is the engineer, directing the train around the corners with his hands on his knees. Once a lap is completed, the player at the front of the train drops

THE TECHNICAL, THE PHYSICAL, AND THE MENTAL GAME

off and assumes the rear pushing position. The rotation continues until all players have pushed for one lap. The first team to finish all four laps is the winning team.

Drill Option

Modify the "Caboose Race" somewhat for players in Peewee or Bantam age groups. Following the same skating format, the first three players are allowed to push opposing teams with one free hand. Each must continue to hold on to the player ahead with one hand, but each one can also make contact with players on opposing teams in an attempt to knock them off balance. Absolutely no punching is allowed. Surprisingly many players completely ignore the goal of the race—to skate fast—because they become so focused on the contact part of the game. This drill often is a great reminder to the players that body contact is only one small part of the game and that the importance of skill, finesse, and teamwork should not be overlooked when it comes to being successful!

Puckhandling

Definition—the skill of having strong and consistent control of the puck using a player's stick and feet

A puck can travel much faster than a player can skate. Players who use passing and team play to generate scoring opportunities demonstrate this principle. However, before a player can pass the puck up to a teammate who is in a more advantageous position, he must gain full control of

the puck or risk a sloppy pass. Consequently puckhandling is an important element of teamwork.

There are two objectives that must be met when performing drills aimed at improving puckhandling. These are

1. *increasing the distance of stick movement from side to side, and*
2. *ensuring proper body weight transfer.*

Increase the Distance of Stick Movement from Side to Side

All players have practiced cushioning the puck with their sticks and keeping their heads up when handling the puck. These are important for effective puckhandling. However, an important, often overlooked aspect of effective puckhandling is the width of the area used. Even though many young players feel confident when handling the puck, they also unfortunately have a span of stick movement that covers only one or two feet. These players can be more easily poke checked and often find it more difficult to maneuver around opposing defensive players. As a result, it is important that all puck-handling drills encourage puck movement from side to side that is as wide as possible, so that one-on-one coverage becomes more difficult and so that players become more skilled at avoiding pressure from the opposition. Encouraging players to widen out their puckhandling movements in all drills during practice will slowly ensure improvement. Drills such as "Attack the Triangle" (page 36) are specifically designed to work on this hockey skill.

Ensure Proper Body Weight Transfer

Many experts believe that the key to skillful puck movement is proper weight transfer. Many professional players can pass and shoot without weight transfer because of their highly developed upper body strength; however, young minor hockey players do not have that same level of experience or strength.

When teaching young players the correct way to pass and shoot, weight transfer from rear to forward foot must be mastered first during puckhandling drills. This can be accomplished simply by having the players stickhandle in a stationary position. Coaches can observe each player to see if they are transferring their weight from one foot to the other while moving the puck back and forth. Similar but progressively more complex weight transfer techniques can be used when advancing from puckhandling to passing and finally to shooting the puck. The skill of proper weight transfer therefore must be an integral part of teaching a young player to handle the puck.

Great players in the National Hockey League control the puck fluidly during their skating stride, all while skating at top speed. This combination of increased stick movement and weight transfer all at top skating speed takes a great deal of high intensity practice. Coaches can begin this learning process by emphasizing these two objectives in every puckhandling drill.

KEYS TO EFFECTIVE PUCKHANDLING DRILLS

Puckhandling is a fundamental skill in almost every aspect of games and practice drills. Therefore, it is important to encourage players to cushion the puck with an angled stick in every drill where pucks are used. Even in skating drills where pucks are not used, it is important for players to keep their sticks close to the ice during skating strides so they become accustomed to controlling the puck with speed. During a forceful forward stride remind players to thrust their sticks in front of them close to the ice. The forward and backward movement of the stick attained during the skating stride keeps the stick blade closer to the ice for a potential pass and also produces more forward momentum while skating. As with all skills, puckhandling drills should progress to a high intensity, simulating game situations as much as possible.

My first major international hockey experience occurred in 1979 during the prestigious Rude Prava tournament in Prague, Czechoslovakia. I was a member of Canada's Olympic Team scheduled to play the national teams from Russia, Czechoslovakia, and Sweden. I had never played against the Russians, but like most Canadians I had watched them in the 1972 Canada-Russia summit series. The Russian team still had some great international stars, including Tretiak, Maltsev, Kharlamov, and Mikhailov. As great as those players were, the one who impressed me most was big number 15, Alexander Yakushev. A beautifully fluid skater, Yakushev reminded many people of the Mahovlich brothers because of his size and grace. As a right defenseman against this big Russian left-winger, what I remember most was his incredibly wide puckhandling span. It almost looked as if he could handle the puck from one side of the rink to the other, and do so with the grace of a ballerina. He was no stronger, faster, or tougher than the other Russian players, but his amazing puckhandling skill set him apart from the rest!

DRILL FAVORITE FOR PUCKHANDLING

Attack the Triangle

This drill is designed to develop effective, wide movement of the puck.

Objectives

- to stickhandle at close quarters
- to encourage wide puck transfer during stickhandling

Key Teaching Points

- Exaggerate stickhandling.
- Keep head up when stickhandling.

Description

Divide the players into pairs and have the pairs spread out on the ice. One player holds a stick stationary at an angle off the ice such that his or her gloves are about one foot off the ice. The two skates and the stick blade should form a triangle. The second player stickhandles the puck under the first player's stick, attempting to control the puck perfectly. The puckhandler's stick must come up and over the stationary stick during each puckhandling movement. The stationary player watches the puckhandler's eyes. If the puckhandler is consistently looking down, then the stationary player reminds him to look up. The players switch positions after one or two minutes. During this drill, the emphasis should be on achieving the greatest distance possible in side-to-side puck movement.

Drill Option

A good progression for "Attack the Triangle" is one where players puckhandle around the perimeter of the ice while the coach tries to poke check them. Each player tries to move the puck between the coach's stick and feet, thereby attacking the coach's triangle. This is a difficult drill for the players but when mastered it is one more valuable skill learned.

Passing

Definition—the technique of moving the puck from one player to another to obtain a positional advantage

Knowledgeable hockey people have stated that the European influence in hockey has helped to change the game from a "dump and chase" strategy to one of puck control and finesse. It is rightly assumed that it is almost impossible for the other team to score if your team has control of the puck. Improving the skills of speed, agility, and passing are making the game of hockey even more exciting than in the past.

For young players who are just learning the intricacies of the game, passing is a difficult skill both mentally and physically. When a seven- or eight-year-old player has worked hard to get possession of the puck, turning around and giving it up, even to a teammate, is often a tough decision. Players also find it difficult to decide when to pass and when to continue on with the puck. A good rule of thumb that players can can be taught is to always pass to a teammate who is in a better position. A pass without that advantage is a waste of energy and offers the potential for a turnover. If these principles are reinforced consistently and often during practice, then moving the puck to a teammate in a more advantageous position becomes ingrained and players apply the principle instinctively in game situations.

> *...always pass to a teammate who is in a better position.*

The physical skill of passing is similar to that of puckhandling and is the next natural progression in becoming a better hockey player. Skillful puckhandling requires good eye-hand coordination and correct weight transfer. Passing also requires the same effective weight transfer to ensure that a pass is crisp and accurate. As players mature and their upper body strength improves, there may be exceptions to this rule, especially when using a snap pass. However, for younger players, body weight transfer from rear foot to front foot is the key to developing accurate and consistent passing.

Anyone who has seen Wayne Gretzky play has marveled at his uncanny ability to pass through traffic right onto the stick of a teammate. As a former teammate I have been on the receiving end of hundreds of his passes. What amazed me was not just that he was aware of each player's ice position or that he successfully completed the pass when opposing players surrounded him. The most impressive aspect of his passing game was that virtually every pass he made landed flat on the ice, easy to receive or make a one-time shot. His stick was heavy with a wide, straight blade but for Wayne it was like a magical spoon dishing off those amazing feeds to any of his teammates in the open.

KEYS TO EFFECTIVE PASSING DRILLS

Hundreds of passing drills are available to develop players' passing and receiving skills. Two basic keys to effective passing drills are:

1. Skate them at high tempo. As with the majority of drills, one key to effectively performing passing drills is that they should be skated at high tempo. Becoming a good passer while standing still or skating at half speed benefits a player minimally because, in a game situation, it is unlikely a player will ever have the opportunity to pass from a standstill. Also, if players are only working at half speed, then stop and change the drill. A drill is a waste of time if it develops habits that produce poorer hockey players!

> *...one key to effectively performing [passing] drills is that they should be skated at high tempo.*

2. Include as many players as possible. Using many players in a drill is much more effective than having the majority standing around and waiting to take a turn. A drill that allows eight players to skate and pass simultaneously is twice as efficient as one where only four players at a time participate.

> *Drills should include as many players as possible...*

It may be difficult to organize every practice drill where most of the players are constantly skating. Unfortunately, there are some effective drills that require one-on-one instruction and skill development. In these drills it is worthwhile to divide the team into two or three subgroups, each led by an assistant coach who runs specific individual drills at different stations on the ice. The players rotate through each of the stations every few minutes and stay much more active during practice than if they were in one large group.

DRILL FAVORITE FOR PASSING

Four Corner Box Passing

During this drill a large number of players are actively working on their receiving and passing skills. Players must stay mentally sharp during the drill because of the quick player rotation required to maintain an effective drill.

Objectives

- to make and receive passes with good cushioning technique
- to skate hard to the net for a shot and possible rebound
- to quickly rotate positions once a pass has been completed

Key Teaching Points

- Give a good target in anticipation of a pass.
- Attempt to receive a pass with control and quickly release the next pass.
- Skate at full speed as the first passer and during the drill rotation.

Description

Divide players and goalies into two groups, one located at each end of the rink. The players line up in one corner of the rink facing the blue line. One player is positioned on the face-off dot just outside the blue line on the near side of the ice, another on the blue line dot on the far side of the ice, and finally a third player is located on the corner face-off dot directly opposite the side where the remaining players are lined up.

The first player in line begins skating and then passes a puck to the player on the near blue line dot. The puck is quickly passed to the player on the far blue line dot and then back into the offensive zone to the player on the corner face-off dot. During those passes, the first player skates around the first passer and directly through the middle of the ice back towards the net. That player then receives a pass from the third passer and advances to the net for a shot.

To complicate the drill and challenge the players mentally, add a positional rotation. The shooter immediately goes to the corner face-off dot. That player moves up to the far blue line dot position. The player in that position skates quickly over to the near blue line dot and the player in that position follows the shooter to the net looking for a rebound. At the completion of the play, the trailing player then takes

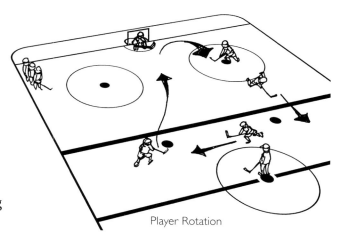

Player Rotation

the puck to the end of the corner lineup, waiting for the next turn.

Drill Options

Organized properly, this drill promotes high-paced, quick-release passing and receiving between several teammates. There are two progressions of this drill that will challenge players to become even more effective passers.

1. Have all players receive and pass the puck on the backhand. This will encourage them to practice a skill that most hockey players spend little time working on.

2. Have all players attempt saucer passes, where the puck is passed through the air with a spinning motion, landing on the ice just before it reaches the pass receiver.

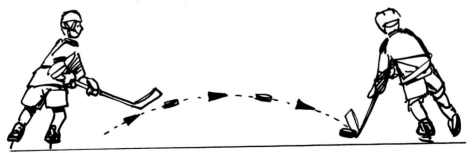

Shooting

Definition—the skill of propelling the puck towards the goal with a stick

For many young players the most enjoyable aspect of hockey is shooting. Just watch a youngster on the ice before practice or on an outdoor rink. Given a net or section of the boards in a rink, children could spend all day practicing their array of shots. The level of interest or commitment is not quite the same when it comes to doing agility or power drills. It is no wonder that kids love to practice shooting. It is an action that provides the most concrete and immediate feedback—goals—and is related to success in game situations. It is also the most fun. These are good reasons why it is necessary to spend time teaching the proper way to shoot the puck. There are whole books that describe the various types of shots—wrist shot, backhand shot, one-footed snap, two-footed snap, and slap shot. Instead of describing the various shots, however, this section focuses on two essential components of skillful shooting—weight transfer and release speed.

Weight Transfer

There is a natural progression of weight transfer from puckhandling to passing. That progression applies just as naturally to shooting, since the most important element of a hard, accurate shot is effective weight transfer. Once players feel comfortable shifting their weight from one leg to the other while puckhandling and passing, strong wrist shots follow quite naturally.

It is obvious when looking at the human body that the leg muscles are much bigger and stronger than

the arm muscles. It naturally follows that coaches can use this fact to entice players to shoot using their whole bodies, not just their arms. After all, when attempting to use a wrist shot, backhand shot, two-footed snap shot or slap shot, body weight transfer is the key to making a strong, accurate shot. Only the one-foot snap shot does not involve body weight transfer and, for the most part, only elite players and those competitive players over the age of sixteen have sufficient upper body strength to execute this shot properly.

Coaches often discourage young players from using a slap shot during practices or games only to receive a stunned look of disbelief. After all, the pros use slap shots all the time; they score a lot of goals with them! Unfortunately young players do not realize that the professionals mastered the art of proper weight transfer with puckhandling, passing, and wrist shots long before they began working on a slap shot technique. Many youngsters try to master the slap shot simply by swinging their stick at the puck, not learning the proper technique at all. Weight transfer from rear to forward leg is just as important for a slap shot as it is for an effective wrist shot. A slap shot is indeed a valuable shot for many players; however, it must develop from the proper progression from previously learned skills.

A former teammate, Mark Messier, seems to have patented a particular type of shot that works well for him. As Mark skates down the right wing (his off wing) he extends back on his inside left leg and lets fly a snap shot that often catches goalies flatfooted and moving across the crease. Using no weight transfer, Mark relies on his muscular forearms to propel the puck so quickly. I have often watched young players try to emulate this unique shooting style, generally without much luck. They just have to wait for a few more years, a lot more muscle, and thousands of practice repetitions!

Release Speed

The component of shooting that is often overlooked in many hockey skill manuals is that the speed of a shot is not as important as the speed with which a player releases the shot. A slow loping back swing causes many blocked shots and easy plays for the opposition since the goalie has time to properly prepare for the shot. In practice, encourage players to release their shots quickly in every drill and even perform drills where they must shoot off balance.

A great drill for improving shot release speed is the "Breakaway Race," where players are encouraged to skate as fast as they can towards the net, always keeping their feet moving. Most players will begin to coast in preparation for their shot, an obvious clue for the goalie to become fully prepared. When shooters skate quickly all the way to the net, they become accustomed to revealing their shooting intentions very late, often freezing the goalie in the net and making a glove or blocker save more difficult.

KEYS FOR EFFECTIVE SHOOTING DRILLS

Although players do not realize it, they practice shooting every time they handle or pass the puck. Therefore, shooting drills should progress naturally from puckhandling and passing. Emphasize the importance of a

Coach John Muckler of the Oilers got very frustrated one year at the extraordinary number of rebound opportunities that our forwards were missing from in front of the opposition goal. He noticed that our players would take a shot and frequently curl away from the slot area, effectively taking themselves out of scoring position. Although he never mentioned this habit specifically, for a two-week period at practice, John constantly reminded us to continue skating hard to the net looking for rebounds after taking the initial shot on goal. Pretty soon he didn't even have to mention it, as it seemed that all the players had quickly broken this bad habit and replaced it with an improved offensive shooting and rebounding technique, all because of effective coaching and frequent repetition!

quick release and follow-up skating directly to the front of the net to look for potential rebounds.

Too frequently during shooting practice players will take a shot on goal and immediately skate to the end of the player lineup in the corner of the rink. This habit is repeated many times throughout each practice with no emphasis on the potential for a rebound and the resulting secondary scoring chance. Invariably during a game, these players will instinctively skate directly by the slot area after a shot, just as they have done hundreds of times before in practice, only to miss out on a glorious scoring opportunity from a rebounded puck lying directly in front of the net!

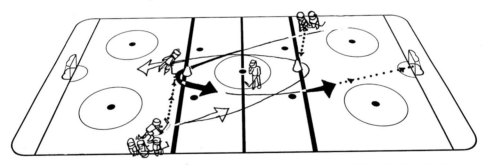

DRILL FAVORITE FOR SHOOTING

Full Ice Horseshoe Drill

The "Full Ice Horseshoe Drill" is probably the one in my drill manual that I use most because of its high tempo, its ability to involve many players, its great progressions, and its direct application to game situations. It is designed to help players progress from passing and puckhandling to effective shooting on goal.

Objectives

• to receive puck at full speed
• to initiate an offensive attack

Key Teaching Points

- Skate at full speed.
- Concentrate on passing directly onto a teammate's stick blade.
- Initiate good weight transfer with shot.
- Coaches control the drill with a whistle.

Description

Divide players into two groups with each group positioned on opposite ends of both blue lines with pucks. Set up pylons in the middle of both blue lines. Start the drill with a whistle. The first player in each line skates hard around the far blue line pylon. After turning back towards his original end, he receives a pass from the player at the front of the opposing line and then skates quickly for a shot on goal and a possible rebound after entering the offensive zone. Once each player receives a pass, blow the whistle to signal the next two players to begin the drill. This drill can be run at a high tempo, with coaches controlling the flow with a whistle. If there is a bad pass or if a player falls, then delay the next starting whistle until the center ice zone is clear of skaters. Run the drill from both sides of the blue line so that players get a chance to receive and pass the puck in both directions.

Drill Options

1. Send two players from the front of each line on a two-on-zero passing and shooting play or send three players for a three-on-zero attack.
2. Send three skaters on the whistle. One player turns at the center ice dot and becomes a defenseman for a two-on-one challenge.

With an attentive group of players and an alert whistle, it is possible to have fourteen players in

Wayne Gretzky was a master at shooting off balance. Since he was not blessed with a great deal of physical strength, Wayne relied on releasing his shots so quickly that the goalie had little chance to prepare. As you might guess, this is one of the reasons he was such a successful player. Remember that the speed of the shot is not as important as shot accuracy and speed of execution!

action at the same time, using both ends of the rink. There is no standing around during this drill!

Checking

Definition—the skill of confronting an opposing player in order to get possession of the puck

If you mention the word "checking" to a group of young hockey players, in all likelihood, the majority will think immediately of body checking. Though important, body checking is really only a small part of checking. Checking is a skill that is used hundreds of times during a game, even in games with young players where the rules disallow body contact. Checking includes angling a player to the boards, poke checking, sweep checking, one-on-one defensive positioning, shoulder and hip checking. Only the last two always involve physical contact.

Teaching young players all forms of checking is an integral part of their development. Using checking drills that are neither intimidating nor physically harmful is a great way to help players become comfortable with checking, even though they may not yet have experienced full contact hockey. In minor hockey organizations where body checking begins at higher levels, it is important to build young players' confidence in their checking techniques. It is a valuable way to prevent the high player dropout that regularly occurs at the age levels where full contact is allowed. In the case

Angling

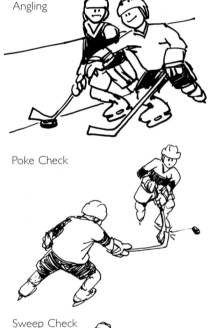

Poke Check

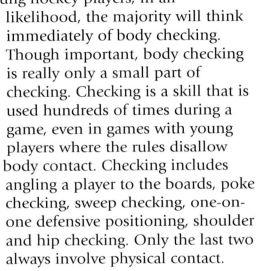

Sweep Check

of players with smaller stature, the introduction of checking is a common reason for these youngsters to quit hockey and turn to other potentially less intimidating activities.

One-on-One
Defensive Positioning

KEYS TO EFFECTIVE CHECKING DRILLS

The two areas of skill development that are most neglected by coaches in lower levels of hockey, are goalie skills and effective checking techniques. Introduced properly, checking drills can allay the fears of many young players and show them valuable ways of separating the opposing player from the puck. Consider these three keys to teaching checking skills:

Shoulder Check

1. *Maintain drill control.*
2. *Teach checking early.*
3. *Emphasize the ultimate reason for checking.*

Hip Check

Maintain Drill Control

It is a pleasure to see a young player who is initially apprehensive about checking begin to feel comfortable with, learn, and even enjoy on-ice checking drills. For developing young players it is essential to use a slow progression, beginning with simple angling drills done at controlled speeds to ensure that no injuries occur and that player confidence is developed slowly.

Teach poke checks and sweep checks first, as these emphasize positional technique rather than physical contact. Then progress to controlled shoulder and hip checks. By ensuring that all players are working

When playing against the Edmonton Oilers in the 1980s, many opposing teams adopted a strategy of dumping the puck deep into the offensive zone and forechecking with full pressure. The thinking was that if they could keep the puck from being passed up to our skilled forwards, then there would be fewer chances for us to score. This meant, of course, that our defensemen were often rattled up against the end boards by the opposing forwards. Mark Messier once approached me after a particularly rough game and asked why I didn't keep my elbow up so that opposing forwards would slow down a bit as they came at us. I replied that I didn't mind taking a hit because I was almost always able to release my pass before being slammed against the boards. Getting the puck up to our skilled forwards was my job and once that was done I was willing to take the hit in order to make a good play. And with all the equipment I wore, it may have sounded like a bone crunching hit, but it didn't really hurt. Also, the forechecking winger's momentum tended to take him out of the play for a longer time, so our breakouts were more successful. We had a motto in the dressing room, "You gotta take a hit to make a play!"

on technique rather than trying to smash their teammates through the boards, coaches can teach players of all sizes and abilities to be more comfortable with this important part of game.

Teach Checking Early

It is common for minor hockey organizations to hold checking camps or special programs for players just before they enter the level where full contact checking is allowed, usually at age twelve or thirteen. However, it is a significant oversight to omit teaching checking skills to young players.

Players should be exposed to basic checking techniques as soon as they can skate. An angling drill, for example, does not hurt them or their teammates but allows them to gain a level of comfort with limited physical contact early in their hockey experience. As these young players progress, they have a distinct advantage over players who are only exposed to physical pressure and player contact at higher age levels. The keys to successfully teaching checking early are that the coach uses fun drills and that he has total control so that no player gets hurt.

Emphasize the Ultimate Reason for Checking

When players are asked the purpose for checking, the answer often is "to hit them hard" or "to intimidate the other team." For this reason it is important that coaches, parents, and administrators support the position that there is only one real reason to check an opposing player—to get control of the puck. If a player body checks an opposing player and does not end up with the puck, then that is an ineffective play. At higher levels of hockey many less skilled players are motivated to continue playing because they like retaliating with monster checks—"to make him pay." There is no place in the game for this attitude and coaches must enforce a policy of zero tolerance for any display of this sort of behavior.

DRILL FAVORITE FOR CHECKING

One-on-One Stationary Keepaway

This drill is designed to increase a player's confidence in engaging in aggressive physical contact and to develop improved skills in puck protection. The "One-on-One Stationary Keepaway" drill is an opportunity for players to feel more comfortable with physical pressure without worrying about being injured or intimidated.

Strong Shoulder

Objective

- to develop proper body positioning and stability while protecting the puck when physical pressure is applied

Players should be aware that one side of the body is stronger than the other side simply because of the extra length of stick and blade extending past the hand. The extra leverage of the stick ensures that the protector can more easily control the opponent's movements going around him from both sides, effectively setting up a wider barrier to go around in order to reach the puck.

Key Teaching Points

- Control the opposing player off the strong shoulder (arm gripping the lower part of the stick).
- Use a tripod stance with stick on the ice and knees bent to maximize stability.
- Coaches ensure maximum intensity by controlling the drill with the whistle.

Description

Pair up players according to size and ability. Each pair has one puck that is left motionless on a designated spot on the ice. While facing the puck, one player protects it from the opponent at his back. The puck protector tries to keep the other player off his strong shoulder.

By positioning an opposing player more closely to the strong shoulder than the weaker side, a player gains an advantage during a one-on-one challenge. The opposing player can pivot, turn, and move laterally in order to get close to the puck and move it. Begin and end the drill with a whistle, so that the timing of the challenge is short and of high intensity. Each one-on-one challenge should last no longer than five seconds.

Drill Options

1. As players become comfortable using their bodies to protect the puck, increase the difficulty of the drill by removing the stick of the protecting player. This challenges the protecting player to be more stable and aware of the opponent's movements.

2. Have two defenders protecting the puck from one opponent.

3. Advance the drill to a two-on-two battle for the same puck.

Positional Play

Definition—the skill of being in proper position on the ice during game situations

Once a young player has mastered the basic individual hockey skills, the next natural step is to begin team-oriented learning. Positional play is a critical ingredient of a successful team and specific practice drills are vital to ensure that the players get a good understanding of this component of hockey.

KEYS TO EFFECTIVE POSITIONAL PLAY DRILLS

Keep positional drills effective by following these key points:

1. *Progress step by step.*
2. *Expose players to all positions.*

Progress Step by Step

It is not uncommon for inexperienced coaches to try to teach six- or seven-year-olds exactly where their feet should be, who they should be looking at, and how their sticks should be held when they are in specific defensive position situations. Although it may be possible for a twelve- or thirteen-year-old to understand these aspects of positional play, it is far too abstract a concept for very young players. It is necessary to introduce positional play in a slow, progressive way so that young players do not become overwhelmed.

For beginners, the first step is to simply skate hard and follow the movement of the puck, with little emphasis on specific positions. Next, teach players how to stay on one side of the ice— the right winger stays on the right side of the ice, the left winger stays on the left. Further instruction may include teaching players how to follow the puck movement up and down the ice while staying on the proper side of the rink, thus establishing an early understanding of five-player team movement. Once these skill levels have been mastered, it is then possible to instruct players on specific defensive and offensive zone positioning, foot alignment, stick preparedness, and other more intricate skills.

> We had a saying in the Oilers dressing room, "There's no 'I' in team." We often used it to remind ourselves that hockey is a team game and that it takes every player in the lineup to produce a successful effort.

If these skills are taught progressively as players are capable of learning them, then their understanding will likely be greater and their ability to use them in a game will be enhanced.

Expose Players to All Positions

At every hockey school where I have instructed, there always seems to be at least one player who approaches the instructors and states, "I'm a right winger and that's all I want to play." Imagine a student at school saying to a teacher, "I am only good at mathematics and that is all I want to study!"

It is natural for parents and coaches to want to see players succeed in their sporting pursuits. However, if they considered for a moment what they truly want for a child as a whole person, then they would realize how important it is to expose players to every hockey position, especially before they reach ages twelve or thirteen. Can a left winger possibly be the best at that position without knowing what the defensemen and center are thinking in a variety of game situations?

The ability to understand, anticipate, and react to a given situation is a fundamental requirement of a great hockey player. Therefore, playing youngsters in every skating position provides a valuable learning experience that cannot be gained in any other way.

> *...realize how important it is to expose players to every hockey position...*

The flip side is that rotating players may lead to early confusion and thus to a less consistent effort on the ice. There is always the potential that the confusion could produce losses in a few games that the team may have otherwise won. However, coaches must ask themselves this most important question—Is winning the highest priority or is it to make players the best they can be?

Changing players to different positions on the ice during games and practices can be a coaching challenge. There will be resistance from many parents, as well as possibly from some of the players. It is important to convey to both groups the ultimate reason for such decisions and what you are trying to accomplish.

There are several available options for effective player rotations. Players can be rotated randomly each shift, with no assigned positions for any players during the game. This option works best for very young players who have not yet learned the concept of offensive and defensive zones or right and left halves of the ice. Player positions can be changed each period, every game, or partway through the season. Most importantly, it is crucial that the players and parents are a big part of such a

When I was coaching my son in Atom hockey a few years ago, I gave all the players the option of playing the same position all year or regularly rotating. Luckily it ended up that one set of five players wanted to play only one position while the others were prepared to experiment and rotate throughout the year. Interestingly, by the end of the year all five "one position" players had asked to rotate through all positions like their teammates because it looked like more fun and a bigger challenge!

THE TECHNICAL, THE PHYSICAL, AND THE MENTAL GAME

Clare Drake, coach of the University of Alberta Golden Bears hockey team, used to be almost fanatical about practicing specific team positional drills. I remember wondering why he did not have a wide variety of drills that he could use during practice to teach us proper positioning but also make practice a little less tedious. After all, Coach Drake was reputed to be one of the best hockey coaches ever. I kept questioning this rather boring practice repetition until I saw how well our team came together as a unit, ultimately winning conference titles and national championships. I should have known that Coach Drake had made these types of drills a priority because they were the best ones to lead our team to success.

decision so that all involved look upon any positional changes as a positive step.

DRILL FAVORITE FOR POSITIONAL PLAY

Defense to Wing to Center Breakout

This drill is designed to develop a consistent, safe, and effective defensive zone breakout pattern for players of all ages. Many coaches believe that it is the foundation for almost all other breakout patterns in hockey. As such, this drill is a favorite for many coaches of all age groups.

Objective

- to develop proper defensive zone positioning
- to develop an effective team breakout system

Key Teaching Points

- Defense looks for teammate position before reaching puck.
- Winger has back to boards, facing the whole ice surface.
- Make passes directly onto teammate's stick.

Description

Players line up at the inside edge of the defensive circle at both ends. One player starts as a winger and begins at the defensive face-off dot. The coach starts the play by dumping the puck into the corner. The first player in the line, the defensive player, retrieves the puck as the winger skates quickly to the boards.

The defensive player passes the puck to the winger, while the center swings below the face-off dot for a second pass. Once the center receives the pass, he skates quickly to the opposite end of the rink for a shot on goal.

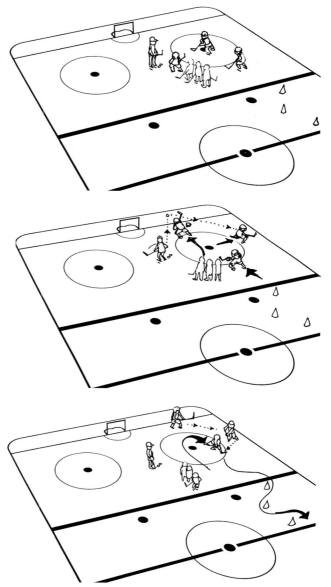

Add several pylons in the neutral ice zone to develop a stickhandling component to the drill. Once the drill is completed, the defensive player then becomes winger and the winger becomes the next center. This process is repeated until all players have rotated through all three positions several times at both ends of the rink.

Encourage players to use proper timing so that when the center curls low in the defensive zone for the second pass, it is made directly across from the winger. This way there is no tendency for the center to get too far ahead of the play where receiving passes becomes more difficult and a pinching defenseman becomes more dangerous. A controlled breakout with five skaters participating is much more effective than one where the players are scattered all over the ice!

Drill Option

This drill is one of the most important fundamental drills in hockey. It is designed to give teams practice on easily exiting their defensive zone with full control of the puck. To reinforce how important it is for wingers and centers to stay deep in the zone, an opposing defenseman can be added to the drill. The defenseman attempts to pinch in from the blue line once a pass is made from the corner. With a simple three-meter diagonal pass to the center who is wide open, all players will gain confidence in using this breakout system.

Intuition

Definition—the skill of properly anticipating how the play will progress in the next few seconds during a game

There are many great players in the National Hockey League and each has characteristics that make him valuable to their teams. Some may be physically dominating like Mark Messier or Mario Lemieux; others, quick and agile like Sergei Fedorov and Paul Kariya. All of the great players in the NHL have one quality in common, however. Each superstar and to some degree every professional hockey player has an uncanny sense of anticipation and awareness of how a play may unfold. In some cases players seem to be born with this intuition. Wayne Gretzky has often been described as having this natural intuition because of his amazing hockey skills. More commonly though, a strong intuitive sense is honed through repetitive practice in game situations or in practice drills that challenge a player to make good decisions about future puck and player movement.

There are many drills that help to develop anticipation and intuition skills; however, one effective way to improve a player's intuition is with shinny hockey. On an outside rink during spontaneous play and without the involvement of coaches, referees, or parents, young players have a valuable outlet to explore new skills. During organized games players often feel apprehensive about trying new techniques or anticipating puck and player movement. During shinny games, however, players can experiment and try new strategies that often require intuitive thinking. When youngsters play shinny frequently during a winter season, they soon become keen intuitive thinkers.

KEYS TO EFFECTIVE DRILLS THAT FOCUS ON INTUITION

There are many players with exceptional physical skills, but only the players with a refined intuitive sense will reach their ultimate potential. From a coaching perspective, it is important to use effective drills that enhance the development of player intuition. Consider the following keys to effective drills for intuition:

1. *Use specific practice organization.*
2. *Use drill progression.*
3. *Use a whistle to control practice.*

Use Specific Practice Organization

In order to help players develop a heightened awareness of events around them, coaches can use the practice drill format to challenge them to be prepared. Many coaches will go over the drills to be used prior to the start of practice, then use name or word cues to switch from one drill to the next. For instance, to start a horseshoe passing drill a coach may elect to simply blow his whistle and say "Horseshoe Drill," and wait for the players to respond. Intuitive players will use this name cue and quickly change position, collect the pucks in the proper area, and then wait for the next whistle to begin the drill. Players who lack this intuitive sense usually end up looking around the ice wondering what to do next. Using this response to practice drill changes is valuable in assessing how a player might be prepared for and respond to certain on-ice situations. Identifying players who lack intuitive skills is the first step toward designing a plan to improve those specific talents.

> *...use name or word cues to switch from one drill to the next.*

Use Drill Progression

Too often a team of young hockey players is exposed to a limited number of drills at practice. This may be because the coach is inexperienced and unfamiliar with a variety of skill-related drills or, in some cases, because the majority of practice time is spent scrimmaging. Constant repetition of drills in practice is important in order to gain a level of confidence and experience in that particular skill area. However, once a skill has been mastered, then practice drills must be modified or changed to further challenge players' abilities. A stationary passing drill, once mastered, should be replaced with a passing drill that also incorporates skating, puckhandling, or shooting the puck. If players are challenged to be aware of slight changes in practice drills, then they will develop a

> *"Those who do not dare to fail greatly fail to achieve greatly."*
> *–Robert F. Kennedy*

heightened intuitive sense as well as decrease the chance of mental and physical stagnation.

Use a Whistle to Control Practice

Practice drills must be carried out in an organized and efficient way. The cost of ice time is the primary reason why hockey has become a rather expensive sport for children, so making most efficient use of time during on-ice practices makes good sense. Coaches should encourage high tempo skating and focus on skill development to get the most out of practice time. Any strategy that better manages the flow of players in practice is 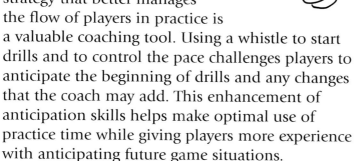 a valuable coaching tool. Using a whistle to start drills and to control the pace challenges players to anticipate the beginning of drills and any changes that the coach may add. This enhancement of anticipation skills helps make optimal use of practice time while giving players more experience with anticipating future game situations.

DRILL FAVORITE FOR INTUITION

Pig in the Middle

This drill is one of my favorites even though there is not a great deal of skating involved. However, the challenge to a player's anticipation, agility, and good passing form compensates for the lack of skating practice. In addition, every player on the team is actively involved at all times—something few other passing drills do. Players work on controlling the puck and quickly redirecting it to another player.

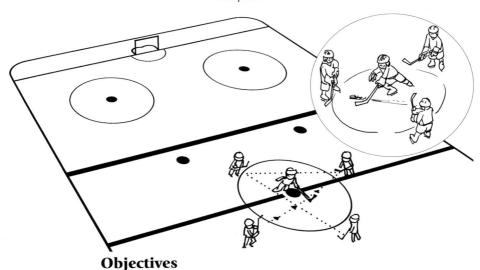

Objectives

- to receive passes well
- to return passes quickly
- to develop high intensity passing skills

Key Teaching Points

- Cushion puck properly.
- Have good stick control.
- Anticipate puck and opposition movement.

Description

Divide players into groups of five or six. Position each group at one of the circles on the ice. One player, the "pig," stays inside the circle, while the others are positioned around the outside of the circle. Using one puck, players must pass through the inside of the circle, while the pig tries to intercept the passes. If the pig intercepts the puck, then the passer becomes the pig and the two switch places. A player who makes a bad pass that cannot be handled properly by the receiver must also become the pig. Encourage players to pass as quickly as they can to stimulate quicker puck movement.

Drill Options

As players develop better passing and receiving skills, it becomes more difficult for the pig to stop the rapid passing. To provide more of a challenge for the passers, try the following progressions:

1. After ten successful passes, players must go down on one knee and continue the game.

2. After an additional ten successful passes, players then go down on both knees.

3. After another ten successful passes, all players must put one elbow down on the ice while still kneeling.

This drill turns the often-tedious aspect of passing practice into a great deal of fun. During the drill the players learn about reactions, anticipation, balance, and puck control. The physical contortions place them in difficult or awkward positions where they still must make an accurate pass to a teammate.

Work Ethic

Definition—the quality that motivates a player to try to perform at the highest possible level

Given enough practice time, capable coaches can teach almost any player how to perform the skills necessary to be a good hockey player. Intuition or a "good head for the game" is also a valuable quality for hockey players of all ages. The final piece of the puzzle in the making of an accomplished hockey player is his or her capacity to

While playing with the Edmonton Oilers in the 1980s, I had the opportunity to play against an enormously talented Swedish player named Kent Nilsson who was the star of the Calgary Flames. We were often more aware of his presence on the ice during Calgary power plays because of his incredible skill handling the puck. The one negative comment that appeared in the media about Kent was his sometimes-lackadaisical effort on the ice, especially during the rough and tumble games when Calgary played Edmonton. In 1987, Kent joined the Oilers and it was interesting to watch his reaction to sharing a dressing room with such superstars as Wayne Gretzky and Mark Messier. Soon after seeing the intensity with which those players approached practices, games, and the preparatory component of the season, we could quickly see an enhanced drive and work ethic coming from this hugely talented player. He became an important part of our Oilers team that beat the Philadelphia Flyers in the 1987 Stanley Cup Finals.

regularly perform at the highest intensity possible.

A strong work ethic by itself is of limited use in the making of an elite athlete, since technical skill, conditioning, and experience form the foundation for an athlete's success. We have all seen young hockey players who love the game and will do almost anything to succeed, but unfortunately cannot match their enthusiasm and dedication with a similar level of skill. These young players usually stop playing organized hockey at age fourteen or fifteen when even recreational teams require a higher skill level and their lack of physical skills becomes a drawback. In contrast, it is also common to see players who have tremendous physical talent and experience but who, unfortunately, are content to play at only half or two-thirds of their potential. This lack of work ethic can easily turn stars into also-rans, and potential Hall-of-Famers into journeyman players who toil for years in the minor leagues.

KEYS TO EFFECTIVE DRILLS THAT PROMOTE A STRONG WORK ETHIC

Consider the following keys to promoting a strong work ethic:

1. *Reward strong effort.*
2. *Organize high intensity practices.*
3. *Use high intensity drills.*

Reward Strong Effort, Not Just Goals and Assists

Inexperienced parents, fans, and some coaches often use individual goals and assists as well as team wins to assess the success or failure of their team. This is an easy mistake to make since the main purpose of the game is to score more goals than the other team. This narrow analysis of success can only be used in one hockey league—the National Hockey League. It is the only league where the very best players have been identified and put together on teams where an ultimate winner can be determined. In the NHL, good play is secondary to whether a team wins or loses, and individual statistics are often used in contract negotiations with team owners.

In minor hockey, however, teams in the same division can have widely varying skill levels, experience, and abilities. A strong team playing a relatively poor game by their standards may still be victorious if they are playing against weaker opponents. If a coach uses winning as the sole criteria for success, then talented players are often rewarded for playing relatively poorly. This kind of inappropriate reinforcement has the potential to develop lazy players who have difficulty telling the difference between a moderate effort and a game played with amazingly strong work ethic. It is up to coaches to give constructive comments after a 9-to-1 win, just as they would give objective praise following a 9-to-1 loss.

> *"Standing around at practice teaches players to stand and watch. High speed skating at practice teaches players to perform with explosive speed."*
> *–Randy Gregg*

It is certainly easier to be the coach of a winning hockey team. There are fewer problems with player motivation and parental concerns, and the dressing room atmosphere is usually more enjoyable. However, because of the very nature of a game in which half of the teams must lose, it is essential that all coaches have a good understanding of how to reward players for good play, not just wins! Those who play in an environment where strong play is rewarded and mediocrity is discouraged learn that sustained intensity and strong effort—work ethic—are key components to achieving their potential as players.

Organize Practices that Encourage High Intensity

Coaches often use on-ice practice time to gather their players together for five or ten minutes to explain certain aspects of team strategy or other complex characteristics of the game. How much more effective might the entire practice be if the coach spends those ten minutes in the dressing

room in front of a chalkboard with more directed attention from the players? The coach gains ten minutes of practice time, more effectively covers the chosen topic, and can initiate an on-ice drill that reinforces the concepts discussed. Most importantly, however, players skate rather than stand around listening. A consistent approach with short, well-organized, high intensity practices can subconsciously establish a positive attitude toward a stronger on-ice work ethic.

Use Drills that Encourage High Intensity

Coaches who instruct their players to skate as hard as they can four times the length of the rink not only deceive themselves but they also teach players to practice working at less than full intensity. Generally in game situations, players are required to use explosive bursts of skating speed for periods of only five to ten seconds at a time, with the rest of the shift comprised of less intense physical actions. Therefore, practicing high intensity drills for longer than ten or twenty seconds is unrealistic and the players ultimately perform them at only 80 or 90% intensity.

> *"Champions in any field have made a habit of doing what others find boring or uncomfortable."*
> *–Anonymous*

Of course, in order to be a good hockey player, one has to maintain a high level of conditioning to sustain performance throughout three periods of a game. Older players, usually after the age of fourteen, can begin aerobic conditioning by training off-ice with hockey-specific drills, riding a stationary bike, or running on a treadmill. For younger players, however, experts agree that formal conditioning is less important and that the bulk of on-ice training should concentrate on individual skill development. Alternative sporting activities such as baseball or soccer in the summer and volleyball or basketball in the winter are great ways to prepare young players for their hockey season.

DRILL FAVORITE FOR WORK ETHIC

Two-on-Two End Zone Challenge

There is no drill that will bring out a hockey player's competitive spirit better than a one-on-one

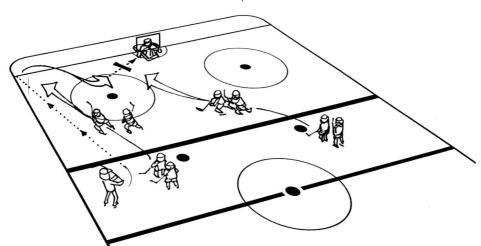

battle for the puck in a game situation. This drill combines a team-focused double one-on-one challenge with an important conditioning component for the players as the drill progresses. The "Two-on-Two End Zone Challenge" fatigues players more quickly than almost any other drill I have seen, yet the intensity comes from within the players rather than from the coaches—the players enjoy the challenge. This drill is also a tool for assessing the level of work ethic that each player possesses, long before a full-ice scrimmage is introduced into practice.

Objective

- to develop strong playing intensity
- to improve offensive and defensive skills
- to improve checking technique

Key Teaching Points

- Encourage aggressive two-on-two with both teams shooting on the same net.
- Anticipate puck movement.
- Point out proper body position for defensive one-on-one challenges.
- Goalie tries to anticipate any shooting opportunity.

Description

Divide players into two groups, one located outside of each blue line facing the offensive goal net. If players are of varying talents on the team, it is wise to separate them into lesser and more skilled groups. A goalie positioned in each net tries to stop both teams from scoring. Further divide each group into two teams randomly and line them up one behind the other just outside the blue line.

To begin the drill shoot a puck into a corner and the first two players on each team skate quickly into the offensive zone to gain possession of the puck. Each team tries to score a goal when it has the puck and tries to prevent a goal when the other team has the puck. This two-on-two challenge continues until the whistle. The players then immediately leave the puck where it lies and skate quickly out of the offensive zone. At the same time, the next two players on each team skate into the offensive zone and begin a second two-on-two challenge.

This player rotation continues for a specified period of practice time until the players begin to show fatigue or the playing intensity begins to drop. It is very important that the player shifts do not last longer than thirty to forty seconds, so that they simulate a regular shift in a game and the players are still able to maintain a high pace of play. Proper rest is vital between shifts to ensure maximal effort. The optimal number of players for this drill is sixteen skaters and two goalies, so that both ends of the rink are used and each team has four players with easy rotations. If a team has fewer skaters at practice, then the drill is best performed only at one end of the ice with all players participating.

Drill Options

To make this drill even more challenging, there are three progressions that can be used effectively.

1. Have a player on each of the two-player teams play without a stick. This challenges them to focus on achieving even better defensive body position and skate blade passing.

2. Have the players use opposite curved sticks (i.e. A left shot player tries the drill as a right shooter) during the drill.

3. Try a three-on-three challenge

A Final Word about Individual Skills

This chapter has provided a great deal of information about individual hockey skills. It is important that all minor hockey players have the opportunity to learn these skills from qualified coaches in a nonthreatening and caring environment. A coaching leader looks far past the team's win/loss record to see if indeed his players have become more successful individuals as a result of regular, well-organized, and efficiently planned drills during practices that are challenging, high paced, and, most importantly, fun!

To sum up:

• Make learning easier by separating hockey skills into their basic components.

• Teach skills progressively; once the players have mastered a particular skill, challenge them with an even more complex drill.

• Be prepared; use on-ice practice time effectively.

• Make practice enjoyable for the players and watch their intensity soar.

The Appendix of this book contains sample practice plans and blank templates to help organize practices from warmup to cooldown. These may be photocopied or adapted to a coach's personal style.

Individual Skills ....Drill Favorites

1. Speed ....Four Corner Circle Relay (p.22)

2. Agility..Shadow Drill (p.26)

3. Power ....Caboose Race (p.31)

4. Puckhandling...........................Attack the Triangle (p.36)

5. Passing...........................Four Corner Box Passing (p.40)

6. Shooting ....Full Ice Horseshoe Drill (p.46)

7. Checking ....One-on-One Stationary Keepaway (p.51)

8. Positional Play .....Defense/Center/Wing Breakout (p.56)

9. Intuition..Pig in the Middle (p.61)

10. Work Ethic.........Two-on-Two End Zone Challenge (p.67)

Chapter 2

3 - Goalie Skills

Whena developing team and individual hockey skills, goalie skills are often overlooked. This is primarily because few coaches have experience in playing the position. Even an experienced head coach who has some valuable input for the goalies often does not have much time to spend one-on-one with these important players. Coordinating drills for the entire team takes precedence. In fact, most minor hockey teams do not even assign a volunteer to be a goalie coach and, as a result, these young players are often left to fend for themselves.

As in the offensive and defensive positions in hockey there are several fundamental skills that every goaltender must develop. These skills include:

1. **Skating**
2. **Agility**
3. **Puckhandling**
4. **Passing**
5. **Positional Awareness**
6. **Up and Down Skills**
7. **Crease Movement**
8. **Glove Skills**
9. **Rebound Control**

NINE KEY GOALIE SKILLS

The first four skills are the same as for any player even though these skills are often used in ways unique to goaltenders. The goalie should therefore work on many of the same drills as the rest of the team, since these team drills are similarly designed to improve a goaltender's overall skill. Later in each practice goalie-specific drills can be included to develop the remaining five skills.

Skating

Young players who have not yet learned to skate well are often asked to play goal, since their lack of skill in skating may not be so obvious in goal and will not be as detrimental to the team. Spectators are likely to notice a speedy winger darting for an open puck to score the winning goal long before they notice how fluidly a goalie plays the angles or how

deftly a goalie controls a puck dumped into the defensive corner. Both of these goalie-specific skills require good skating skills.

The ability to skate well allows goaltenders to cover the corners of the crease more effectively and to become like a third defenseman on dump-ins. They can get to the loose puck and quickly begin the team transition back to offense. One of the most important skills for a goalie is the ability to come out of the crease in order to cut down the angles for oncoming shooters. Strong skaters move more quickly and also keep their pads in better defending position while striding back into the crease in anticipation of a shot or deke.

As players progress into higher levels of hockey, goaltenders have to be some of the strongest skaters on the team simply because of the significantly increased equipment weight! Strong legs and catlike agility allow goalies to move easily throughout the crease area despite their burden of bulky, heavy pads.

I had the privilege of playing in front of some of the best goalies in the National Hockey League. Grant Fuhr, Andy Moog, and Bill Ranford were our main goalies as we progressed through the Stanley Cup playoff rounds. These three successful goalies were completely different in their playing styles, personalities, and attitudes. One characteristic they did have in common was conditioning. Our goalies did all of the same skating drills as the forwards and defensemen throughout the season. I am sure that their commitment to good conditioning was a big reason why these goalies did so well under the pressure of late-season Stanley Cup play.

DRILL FAVORITE FOR SKATING

Skating Philosophy

For goalies, I would like to encourage the development of a skating philosophy rather than an actual drill for skating. During practice, as soon as the skating drills begin, many young goaltenders go to one corner and begin their stretching routine. Although stretching is a valuable practice, many hockey experts believe that goaltenders should be able to do all of the skating drills that the forwards and defensemen perform. In this way young goalies are challenged to attain strong skating speed and endurance, skills that will greatly enhance their netminding pursuits. Once the practice progresses to stickhandling or passing drills for the forwards and defensemen, the goalies have ample time to stretch and warm up, augmenting the early stretching they should be doing even before they step onto the ice.

Agility

No other hockey player is required to go from standing to prone position with as quick and full

recovery as a goaltender must. Skate saves, butterfly maneuvers, stacking the pads, poke check dives—all of these skills require great agility, especially when considering the weight and bulk of goalie equipment. A goalie may have fantastic glove reaction and solid positional play; however, in a dynamic, fast-moving game like hockey where offensive chances often come in multiples, the ability to recover from one play and regain full control for the next is vital. For the netminder, no skill is more important than agility.

Agility is defined as the ability to change directions quickly while maintaining control. The very nature of goaltending demands a high degree of agility, whether recovering to a standing position after a butterfly save or sprawling across the crease to stop a rebound. With the rising cost of ice time, it is advisable to begin showing young goalies simple, inexpensive, and enjoyable drills both on and off the ice that, when done regularly, can improve their agility. An intuitive coach will organize dryland sessions for goaltenders to improve agility, balance, and coordination so that regular ice time can be directed to puck-related skills.

> *For the netminder, no skill is more important than agility.*

DRILL FAVORITE FOR AGILITY

Mirror Drill

The beauty of this simple goaltending drill is that a pair of goalies can perform it at any time during a lull in active shooting or team play. If there is only one goalie at practice, then an assistant coach can easily lead the drill. Fortunately, it is not necessary for a volunteer goalie coach to know much about goaltending skills to organize and encourage the players during this drill.

Objectives

- to develop quick reactions
- to improve agility during specific goaltending maneuvers

Key Teaching Point

- Emphasize speed in both movement and recovery.

Description

Position two goalies facing each other in an area on the ice that does not interfere with the drills the rest of the team is doing. One goalie is the leader and makes quick movements starting from a ready position,

During the 1972 Canada-Russia summit series the Russian National Hockey Program demonstrated how important and effective it is to improve goaltending agility with dryland training. For many years the great Vladislav Tretiak trained aggressively both on and off the ice to gain the amazing strength, endurance, and catlike reflexes that made him a goaltending icon in the hockey world.

simulating those a goalie might use in a game. These movements may include glove save high, blocker save high, stick save low, half butterfly, full butterfly, and so on. The other goalie acts as a mirror, attempting to mimic each and every movement. The coach starts the drill and finishes it after only ten to fifteen seconds so that the goalies don't get overtired, which would prevent them from practicing proper techniques. Once completed, the goalies then switch roles and the drill is repeated.

Drill Option

A coach may lead the drill, with both goalies responding to movements in tandem. This option allows the goalies and coaching staff to see which goaltender has developed better reactions, technique, and stamina.

Puckhandling

It is often assumed that a goalie's responsibility is to stop the puck. Once that is done, then the

defensemen or forwards take over and clear the puck to a teammate or out of the zone. That is often the case with many teams where the goalie has not developed strong puckhandling skills. However, a goaltender who has good puckhandling skills gives the team an added offensive advantage, especially when beginning transitions from defense to offense by controlling the puck adeptly.

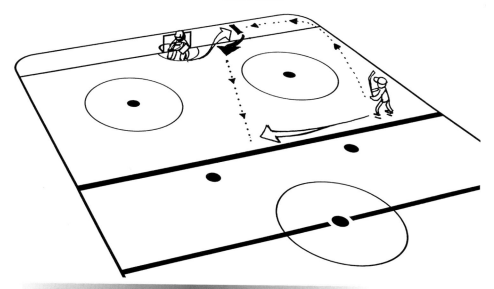

DRILL FAVORITE FOR PUCKHANDLING

Behind the Net Shoot-in Drill

This drill simulates a play that occurs dozens of times during every game when a player dumps the puck around the boards into the offensive zone. The goalie must leave his crease, skate quickly to the boards behind the net, stop and control the puck, and finally either set the puck up for his defenseman or pass it up the ice.

Objectives

- to improve a goalie's reaction to a puck shot behind the net
- to enhance anticipation of this goalie skating movement
- to practice gaining control of a puck moving along the boards behind the net

Key Teaching Points

- Encourage skating speed and anticipation.
- Encourage good puck control.
- Encourage effective clearing passes.

I played in front of two top-notch goaltenders with the Edmonton Oilers in the 1980s. Both Grant Fuhr and Andy Moog provided heroic efforts between the pipes during our Stanley Cup championship years. Confidence, agility, technique, quick gloves, and attitude were only some of the skills that allowed them to dominate their position. However, there was one glaring difference between the two in the way they played the game.

Grant Fuhr was an aggressive butterfly goaltender who loved to come out and challenge shooters. He was also a superb puckhandler. When he had control of the puck we defensemen knew that he would not make a mistake and he would likely set it up perfectly beside the net for us to pick up. Andy Moog was a different story. He was more of a standup goalie who was effective at taking away the shooter's angle. However, when he got control of the puck, we never knew what was going to happen. The Oilers' defensemen were aware of this and whenever he attempted to handle the puck or clear it from the zone, we would often position ourselves near the net just in case a miscue occurred. Weaker puckhandling skills did not hurt Andy's career. In fact, he was one of the greatest goaltenders with whom I had the privilege to play. However, a slight alteration was required in the way his teammates responded to certain situations in order to prevent his occasional dangerous giveaways.

Description

Begin by dumping the puck around the boards into the offensive zone while the goalie is in a ready position in the crease. The goalie quickly skates back to the end boards to stop the puck that is dumped in. Once in control of the puck, the goalie locates the coach somewhere in the defensive zone and makes a clearing pass as quickly as possible. The coach moves around to different positions on the ice to challenge the goalie to be fully aware of player movement throughout the entire defensive zone.

Drill Option

Add a forechecking player to the drill who quickly skates in towards the goalie for additional pressure during the play. This challenges the goalie to be even more aware of the position of teammates who can take passes as well as potential opponents ready to intercept a pass.

Passing

The highlight reels of National Hockey League goaltenders in the 1950s and 60s are always interesting to watch. All great athletes, these goalies played their position almost as if there was a rope tied between their legs and the net. Rarely would they venture far from the confines of their net to handle the puck. Their job was a relatively simple one: just stop the puck when it was shot. With the evolution of a high-speed game involving counterattacks and transition plays in the defensive and neutral zone as pivotal components of the game, the role of a goalie has expanded. A team whose goalie can handle the puck well and start an offensive play with crisp, accurate passes to teammates has a valuable advantage over its opposition. No longer are goalies solely assigned the role of puck stopper; they have become valuable sixth members of the offensive forces.

> *A team whose goalie can handle the puck well and start an offensive play with crisp, accurate passes to teammates has a valuable advantage...*

Unlike defensemen and forwards who usually rely on weight transfer to make hard and accurate passes, a goalie's strategy for passing is slightly different. The angle between a player's stick blade and the shaft of the stick is called the lie. Skating players usually use a lie 5 or 6 stick compared with an almost upright lie 13 goaltender stick. Because goalies have such an upright stick to help stop the puck, it is more difficult for them to sweep the blade of the stick across the ice using proper weight transfer when making a pass. You will notice that goalies will more frequently use a snap pass, using only arm strength to make a quick and accurate pass to a teammate. Very little body weight transfer occurs with a snap pass. This is one of the main reasons why young goalies have a difficult time passing the puck; they have not developed sufficient upper body strength. There are some instances in higher levels of hockey where a goalie will attempt a long distance pass or an end-to-end shot on an open net and will use a weight transfer technique, but this is the exception rather than the rule. Weight transfer when passing the puck is a valuable skill for players in all hockey positions, including goal.

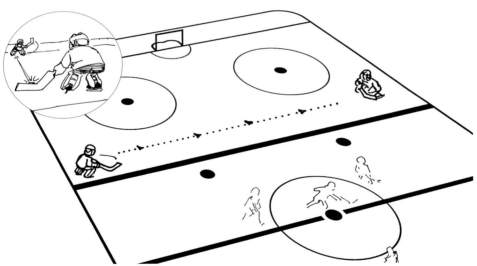

DRILL FAVORITE FOR PASSING

Long Passing Drill

During a practice there are many opportunities for goalie skill development when goalies are not an integral part of the team practice drills, especially during puckhandling and passing drills. This is a perfect time for goalies to pair up across the width of the ice to work on hard, rink-wide passes. Once a goalie feels confident with longer passes that require proper weight transfer and stick control, then shorter defensive zone snap passes will seem easy.

Objectives

- to improve weight transfer passing technique
- to work on accuracy with passing
- to practice puck control when receiving the pass

Key Teaching Points

- Encourage good weight transfer.
- Stress strong stick control with both gloves.
- Reinforce attempts to hit the target accurately.

Description

Two goalies line up across the width of the ice at one end of the rink. Using one puck, each tries to pass it crisply across the ice right onto the stick blade of the opposite goalie. Goalies repeat this maneuver back and forth so they gain confidence in their passing abilities. A contest can be used where one point is given for each pass that hits the target directly. The first goalie to reach five points is the winner.

Drill Option

Once the goalies are proficient in hard cross-ice passes, they can try saucer passes as far across the ice as possible. Using a heel-to-toe spin of the puck and following through high in the air with the stick, they can sail passes through the air to land just in front of the intended target. This is not an easy skill, but one that can come in very handy during a game.

Positional Awareness

Being aware of one's proper position on the ice is a valuable skill for all players, but for goaltenders, this skill is essential. If a forward is caught out of position, a three-on-two play may result. For a defenseman, poor positional awareness may give up a scoring opportunity in the slot area. In the case of goalies, being in the wrong position results in an easy tap-in goal or open net shot that can negatively change the momentum of a game.

It is common to see goalies that shine in practice but have greater difficulty during a fast-paced game. For years they have practiced the same moves, techniques, and strategies that have made them fundamentally strong goalies. Unfortunately, almost all of this experience comes from controlled practice settings, where they are used to having time to properly set up for each shot. Awareness of their location in the net is easy when goalies have ample time to establish where they are in the crease relative to the goal posts.

Good goalies practice what they do well. Great goalies practice what they don't do well!

Great goaltenders often challenge themselves to react in practice to being out of position in order to be better prepared when this inevitably happens in a game. It is interesting to watch one of the best goalies in the National Hockey League, Dominic Hasek. Nobody could ever accuse Dominic of having a methodical, traditional approach to stopping the puck. It is an uncanny awareness of his position in the crease relative to the shooter that allows him to often pull off incredible saves. The situations where he has time to set up and be totally prepared for an oncoming shot become even easier since he is constantly working on his positional awareness.

> At a recent hockey school, I was instructing a group of goaltenders. We were doing the "Spin and Catch Drill" that requires a goalie to face into the net and, after a cue from the coach, spin around to quickly stop a shot. It is a great drill for quickness and agility but also challenges young goalies to become more confident in making saves while off balance or when they are not completely sure of their position in the net. One young fellow had trouble with this drill. Each time he heard the cue he would quickly turn to face me for the shot, but first he banged his stick on the left post and then on the right. He repeated the maneuver and then finally got into his goalie stance. He had obviously learned that it was important to be aware of his position in the crease at all times. The post hitting ritual was a way for him to establish his crease position. This idea may have been a good one except that goalies do not always have time to set up for every shot! The "Spin and Catch Drill" was intended to get him used to stopping pucks when he was not prepared, yet it was difficult to break him of this tedious ritual.

DRILL FAVORITE FOR POSITIONAL AWARENESS

Five Cone Drill

Skating speed and agility are two important skills for goalies; however, they must also confidently traverse from one side of the net to the other as well as easily telescope in and out of the crease, cutting off angles while maintaining good puck-stopping position. The "Five Cone Drill" is a simple drill to organize, but excellent for developing positional awareness.

THE TECHNICAL, THE PHYSICAL, AND THE MENTAL GAME

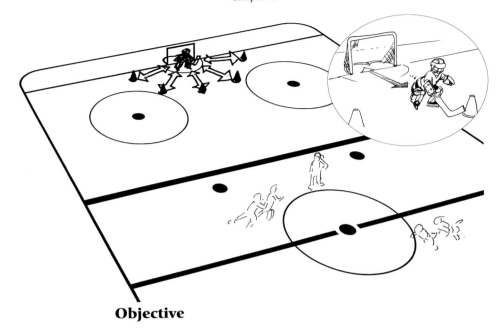

Objective

- to improve a goalie's positional awareness in the defensive zone

Key Teaching Points

- Encourage quick foot movements.
- Practice keeping legs together as much as possible.
- Practice staying in a ready position during skating movements.

Description

Arrange five pylons in a semicircle five meters out from the crease. Spread them out so that one is directly in front of the net, two are at a slight angle and the corner pylons are at a more severe angle from the front of the net. The goalie assumes a ready position in the crease. On a cue from the coach the goalie skates out towards the farthest left pylon and stops in front of it. The goalie then quickly skates backward to regain the proper position in the middle of the crease. This process is repeated for each pylon, until the goalie has skated to and from all five pylons. The goalie may often end up out of position in relation to the net after skating backwards; however, practice will improve the goalie's ability to get back in proper crease position.

Drill Option

When a goalie has mastered the skating component of this drill, the coach can add a shot on net when the goalie returns to the crease after skating backwards from the pylon. This gives the drill a more gamelike flow and reinforces staying in a good puck-stopping stance while skating backwards.

Up and Down Skills

In the more elite levels, goalies must have the ability to make all the routine saves and the majority of the difficult saves. What sets apart the truly great goaltenders from all the rest is the ability to make the game-saving play, which causes a shift in the momentum of a game and thus frustrates the opposition. These plays are successful because the goalie has the ability to recover quickly from a sprawling play or a scramble in front of the crease and return to a standing, ready position.

Up and down skills are especially difficult for young goaltenders because they require good leg strength, which many young players have not yet developed adequately. Therefore, it is important to focus on improving technique while waiting for young muscles to grow in size and strength.

There are two main ways for goalies to get back up to a set position after being down on their knees. Goalies can perform a two-legged hop by pushing down on the front of their skates while forcefully straightening their knees, thus effectively hopping back up to their feet. This is the best technique because it is done at a high speed and goalies stay in better balance during the maneuver.

Younger goalies may not have the leg strength to try this. They often opt for a one-legged method where they first raise one foot properly to be flat on the ice, follow that with an upward body movement, and finally bring the last foot under them in order to rise into a standing position. This is a much slower technique but one that may be used by young goalies or by those who are tired at the end of a high tempo game.

DRILL FAVORITE FOR UP AND DOWN SKILLS

Up and Down Drill

When recovering from a prone or kneeling position, technique and leg strength are required for optimal performance. The "Up and Down Drill" is a simple repetition of the way goalies must maneuver their legs and bodies in order to regain a standing position. A dryland-training program, including squats, can also help to increase functional leg muscle strength and can be done safely by players of all ages. It is not necessary to perform squats using barbell weights to improve leg strength. Proper technique and adequate repetitions can help even young goalies to improve their strength.

Objectives

- to improve recovery time to a standing position from a kneeling position

- to develop better balance following a shot or during a play near the crease

Key Teaching Point

- Emphasize high-speed movement going down and recovering into a standing position.

Description

During practice when there is no active shooting, have both goalies position themselves side-by-side in front of one goal net. On a coach's cue both goalies quickly drop to their knees and immediately stand back up in a ready position. Repeat the movement in sets of three to ten as quickly as possible. Provide a rest period for proper recovery before the next set.

Determine the optimal number of repetitions and sets by the size, age, and ability of the goaltenders but begin with fewer repetitions and sets to emphasize good technique and then slowly increase both as the season progresses. Watch for signs of poor balance during recovery and instruct goalies to try to achieve a more stable body position before trying to hop back up into a standing, ready position.

Drill Options

1. Once goaltenders are proficient at the controlled up and down movement, have them sprawl in a pad-stacking position and then try the quick recovery. Use a stick to indicate the direction the goalies are to stack their pads, thereby ensuring practice on both the left and right sides.

2. Goalies can then try the same drill using a half or full butterfly technique when dropping down.

Crease Movement

The first time hockey players compete on international-sized ice surface, they realize that the

game is much different than on most North American rinks. The forwards love the extra ice in the corners and behind the net because they are havens for nifty puckhandlers and are usually out of the reach of their defensive opposition.

On the other hand, the wider lanes down the side of the boards challenge defensemen. They must adjust their angles for one-on-one plays and odd-man situations. However, it is the goaltenders who have to modify their normal shot setup the most. They have to be aware of cutting down potentially even greater angles and being even more aware of the increased puck movement and play behind the net. With the significant increase in the offensive zone size, goalies must be even more skilled at moving laterally as well as forward and back to counter this apparent offensive advantage. Since the National Hockey League has increased the amount of ice behind each goal line, movement in the crease continues to become an even more important goaltending skill.

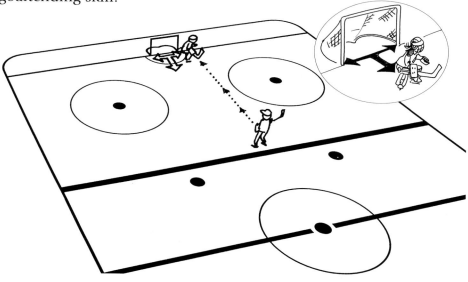

DRILL FAVORITE FOR CREASE MOVEMENT SKILLS

T Drill

This simple drill provides a goalie with practice in moving through the crease with better strength, balance, and speed. Remember, however, that front-and-back movement in the crease is just as important as side-to-side maneuvering. The "T Drill" incorporates both kinds of movement.

Objectives

- to improve lateral and forward/backward skating proficiency
- to gain confidence in aggressively following the puck inside the crease

Key Teaching Point

- Encourage quick movement while maintaining good balance and proper ready position for stopping shots.

Description

Position a goalie with one foot inside a goal post. On a coach's cue, the goalie shuffles from the post to the center of the crease, then skates out to the front edge of the crease. Once at the top of the crease, the goalie stops and skates backward to the goal line, then shuffles to the opposite goal post. Finally, the goalie shuffles back to the center of the crease and tries to stop the puck that the coach shoots. Look for quick skating movement and tight pad control in every part of the T-shaped route.

Drill Option

To increase the level of difficulty in the drill, the goalie skates forward past the crease edge and to a pylon located at the top of the circles. Challenge the goalie with a shot on regaining proper position in the middle of the net.

Glove Skills

One of hockey's most exciting moments is when a goaltender makes a dazzling glove save, robbing the

opposing forward of what was apparently a sure goal. Both blocker and catching gloves are valuable components of a great goalie's defensive arsenal. Although glove speed and quick reflexes are important in developing an intimidating upper body advantage, anticipation and good angling skills are vital for goalies to increase their chances to make great glove saves.

DRILL FAVORITE FOR GLOVE SKILLS

Spin and Catch Drill

When developing improved glove skills, technique is just as important as quick reactions. This drill incorporates a spinning movement followed by a shot to the top corners of the net, challenging goalies to set up and react instantly with either their blockers or catching gloves.

Objectives

- to improve glove catching and blocking skills
- to develop confidence in making saves while gaining balance

Key Teaching Point

- Encourage rapid transition from skating rotation to a ready position for glove saves.

Description

Position a goalie in front of the goal facing backwards into the net. Stand in the high slot in

THE TECHNICAL, THE PHYSICAL, AND THE MENTAL GAME

front of the goal with pucks. Following a cue such as tapping a stick on the ice, the goalie quickly spins around to face forward and moves quickly into a ready position. As soon as the goalie is set, shoot a puck in the direction of either the blocker or catching gloves.

Emphasize the importance of angling the blocker outward so that any rebounds are redirected to the defensive corners rather than back into the dangerous slot area. Repeat the drill five to ten times and then alternate goalies. Always ensure players have adequate rest between drills so that the quality of execution is maintained.

Drill Options

1. Have goalies fall quickly to their knees once they have spun into position on recovering into a ready stance, then shoot a puck to one of the glove sides.

2. Challenge goalies to set up, stack their pads, and then recover for a shot on goal.

3. Challenge the goalies with shots made towards the low corners as well as within reach of their gloves. Goalies must be totally prepared for all shot options using both gloves and pads.

Rebound Control

The vast majority of great goalies rarely get beat on the first shot on goal during a rush. They have the time to set up their angles properly and, unless the opposing player makes a fabulous shot, the advantage certainly is on the goaltender's side. However, once the first save is made, any advantage is negated if the puck is rebounded to the dangerous slot area just in front of the crease. In this situation, opposing forwards have the goalie potentially off balance and unable to prepare easily for a second shot. Although this is where a skilled defenseman can help the

BOINK.

goalie by clearing loose rebounds out of the slot, goalies who are able to minimize dangerous rebounds by directing the puck into the corners are doing themselves a valuable service! As is the case with preventing injuries, preventing a potential scoring opportunity is a great deal more effective than having to react to one. When defensemen and goalies communicate, they can ensure that it is virtually impossible for the opposition to get an "easy goal."

DRILL FAVORITE FOR REBOUND CONTROL

Long Shot Drill

The ability to control rebounds from shots outside the defensive zone is a skill that requires ample practice. Soft, close-in shots can either be smothered under the pads or caught by a catching glove. A long slap shot or wrist shot, however, requires good glove skills coupled with the ability to redirect the puck into less dangerous zones, such as the corners of the rink.

Objective

- to develop confidence in effectively controlling and minimizing rebounds

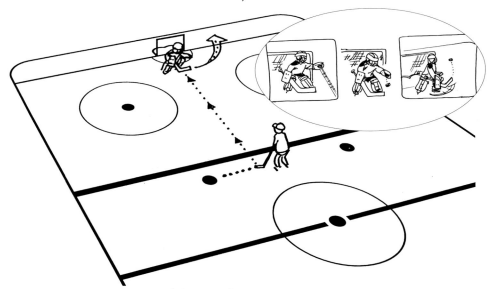

Key Teaching Point

- Emphasize proper body setup—catching glove control and effective angling of the blocker to redirect pucks in the proper direction.

Description

Stand outside the blue line with several pucks. One goalie sets up in the crease. When he is ready, shoot a puck firmly towards the goalie. If the puck hits the goalie's leg pads, then he must try to control the rebound close to his body and sweep it into a corner. If using the catching glove, then the goalie must concentrate on catching the puck smoothly and with good force. He should then drop the puck to the ice, control it with his goal stick and sweep it to one corner. To use the blocker to stop the shot, the goalie should focus on angling his glove in order to redirect the puck to a corner while stopping the shot. Repetition of these skills will increase a goalie's confidence in controlling rebounds!

Drill Options

1. Once goalies have mastered the ability to control rebounds from direct shots, add a twist to the drill

by alternating direct shots with dump-in shots that angle off the corner boards and end up coming in front of the goal. Goalies must learn how to react to dump-ins and be able to control them effectively.

2. Add a defenseman so that rather than simply directing the puck into a corner, the goalie must stop the shot, control it, and set it up beside the net for pickup by the defenseman.

A Final Word about Goalie Skills

In many levels of amateur hockey, goalies are often overlooked when it comes to involving them in practice. Most often this is because the coaching staff do not feel comfortable teaching goalie skills or may not have adequate assistance on the ice during practice. Assigning an assistant coach the responsibility of working with the goaltenders is an effective solution to making sure these important players get the attention they both need and deserve.

There are many skills that young goaltenders need to master in order to reach their full potential. This is only a small sampling of goalie drills that can be used each practice. Another book in the *LifeSport* series, *Hockey Drill Solutions*, provides a comprehensive selection of drills that will make coaching goalies an easy and successful experience.

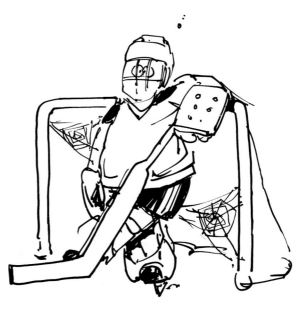

Goalie Skill ························ Drill Favorite

The Physical Game

nutrition, equipment fit,
stretching, injuries, fitness

THE PHYSICAL GAME

I n a demanding contact sport like hockey, many strong, fast, and agile players consistently outperform their equally skilled counterparts simply because of their superior fitness levels. Dryland training programs are commonly used to prepare hockey teams for optimal physical performance. The specific components of fitness and ways to improve in each area are described later in Chapter 8, "Fitness Training—On-ice & Dryland." In addition, good nutrition and hydration, a planned program of sport-specific warmups and cooldowns, properly fitting equipment, and protection from injury all combine to shape the physical part of playing hockey.

Fitness training has progressed very slowly over the years in comparison to the more traditional technical skill components of the game. In the 1960s, professional hockey players had the luxury of coming to training camp and gradually working their way back into shape. A spot on the team was reserved for each of them and the purpose of training camp was to prepare for the upcoming season.

The 90s, however, have spawned a new

era of hockey, where players may get only one or two chances to show their skills and stamina in order to make the team. Although this fact is well known by coaches, managers, parents, and the players themselves, I continue to be amazed at the general lack of fitness evident when some players return from the off-season to begin a new hockey campaign.

This is not to say that young hockey players should play hockey all year round. In fact, I am strongly against summer hockey as there are risks for participants, from both an injury and burnout perspective. Even NHL players who are physically fit, mature, and experienced require an off-season to completely recover from injuries and recharge their batteries, both physically and mentally. It is remarkable how the minor hockey system of today has evolved to such a degree that some young players are being asked to consistently commit to their sport to an even greater degree than is asked of professional players!

We often joked in the Edmonton Oilers dressing room that when our kids got old enough to pick up

a hockey stick, we would take it away from them and give them a tennis racquet or golf club! After seeing the kinds of pressures that exist at a professional level in hockey, we were making the not-so-subtle statement that playing a sport simply for the enjoyment is definitely the best course for young children. I am sure, though, that hockey is no different from other sports, and when tennis players or golfers reach an elite level of play, similar stresses are present. Of course, parents naturally try to make decisions that will ultimately serve their children's best interests.

So what should a hockey parent do when challenged to decide whether to push a child towards more competitive hockey or to just let him or her play recreationally? The decision is not an easy one, since every player has different physical abilities, maturity, focus, and interests. There are, however, guidelines that parents can use to provide direction for budding young hockey players.

International sport medicine experts have recently established guidelines for participation levels for young athletes. These guidelines recommend that children under the age of ten should not participate solely in one sport. A variety of complementary activities are much more effective and enjoyable forms of recreation and development than playing only hockey and lots of it! There has been a significant increase in the number of young athletes with overuse injuries, primarily because of repetitive training in only one sport. Cross training is recommended for improved fitness, and summer sports such as soccer, lacrosse, or baseball are great alternatives to summer hockey. Whatever parents and their child decide regarding competitive or

> In our clinic I see many hockey players with overuse injuries. I often talk to their parents about the importance of a balanced approach to all sports, including hockey. Frequently a parent's response is, "But he just loves playing and, if we let him, he would play ten hours a day!" My response to that comment is often that my children would love to stay up until midnight every night and watch television, but as parents, my wife and I make the decision to get them to bed at a reasonable hour, because that is best for them! It is important that parents and coaches help players achieve a healthy balance in their lives since many cannot do it themselves because they lack experience.

recreational hockey, it is imperative that coaches, parents, and especially players keep in mind the potential risks of focusing too narrowly on one specific sport at a young age.

This section of the book provides information for both coaches and parents on those physical aspects of hockey that, though they may not relate directly to the game, provide the foundations for development of the ultimate player. The coach who provides players and their parents with information on and opportunities for fitness training, good nutrition and hydration, a stretching program, equipment fitting and maintenance, and protection from injuries is setting the stage for a winning team, and not just on the scoreboard!

4 - Nutrition & Hydration

L ike many other highly competitive athletes, hockey players are constantly trying to gain an advantage over their competition. It is now well known that proper nutrition and hydration can provide a natural performance enhancement for enlightened hockey players.

In the past players paid little attention to what they ate and drank before, during, and after games. It was assumed that skill and conditioning were the most important determining factors in the development of great hockey players. When players were fatigued at the end of a game, they assumed it was a natural result of working hard for 60 minutes.

It wasn't until the mid-1980s that hockey coaches, managers, and players began to consider the importance of proper nutrition and hydration for optimal performance. Interestingly, hockey lagged far behind other sports, especially when compared to the significant advances being made in sports like track and field, soccer, and swimming at that time. However, hockey is catching up. In fact, optimal nutrition and hydration before, during, and after competition is becoming well known and practiced at every level of hockey.

Fuel for Hockey

Hockey is a dynamic, fast-paced sport requiring the best available energy during the one or two hours of a practice or a game. Energy comes from what we eat and drink, as well as from how the energy systems in our body use these nutrients. Although it is assumed that young athletes learn about proper nutrition in school, they often make fundamental mistakes when choosing pregame foods. That is why it is important for coaches to have a good understanding of how both good and poor nutrition impact the performance of the athletes under their direction.

The human body acts like a gas-powered engine. The engine requires fuel, air, and a spark to ignite the fuel burning process. The human body similarly needs fuel in the form of nutrients, air from our lungs, and enzymes and chemicals in the muscles to begin the process of muscle movement. Like an engine, the body produces heat when active, and this heat must be eliminated by sweating. Bodies with weaker muscles are unable to move effectively. Bodies that cannot take in enough oxygen through the lungs also cannot perform optimally. Finally, bodies that do not have good stores of fuel cannot perform at peak levels during competition.

In this chapter I describe the six major nutrients required by the body, their function, and the foods that provide these nutrients. In addition I have provided pregame and postgame strategies for good nutrition. It is worthwhile for coaches to encourage their players to use these nutrition strategies for peak performance in games and practices. The knowledge will also serve them well in their future sport and life endeavors.

There are six major nutrients required for good health and for ideal athletic function.

1. **Carbohydrates**
2. **Fats**
3. **Proteins**
4. **Minerals**
5. **Vitamins**
6. **Water**

CARBOHYDRATES

Carbohydrates are the compounds in food that are the primary providers of the energy required for intense activity such as that required for playing hockey. Most of the day's calories (60–70%) should come from these energy sources. Carbohydrates are stored in the working muscles of the body as well as in the liver as glycogen. When carbohydrates are depleted from the muscles during

In the 1980s, the Quebec Nordiques were still a franchise in the National Hockey League. It was well known around the league that their building, The Colisée de Québec, was home to the best hot dogs anywhere on the circuit. Players would often stop in after the pregame skate to sample a couple of the treats they fondly called "chiens chaud," as they were known throughout the league. Players might also have one of these famous hot dogs right before the game if they were particularly hungry. One player famous for this habit was Wayne Gretzky. Of course, after downing these less than nutritious "chiens chaud," Wayne would often go out and score a couple of goals and get a bunch of assists to lead our team in scoring. We all marveled at his athletic prowess and knack with the puck. However, I have often wondered how much greater he might have been if he had used good pregame nutrition to his advantage during those early years!

activity (after about an hour), the body reacts by releasing more from the liver and distributing them throughout the body via the blood stream. Sources of carbohydrates include fruits, vegetables, and grains; the latter is a category that includes such foods as pasta, bread, pancakes, cereals, and rice.

FATS

Fats are an important energy source particularly for prolonged low-intensity activity. A small amount of fat is also needed in order for the body to function properly. The recommended level is about 20 to 25% of the calories in a performance enhancing

diet. Most of this fat should come from unsaturated fat sources such as vegetable and fish oils.

Unfortunately, North American diets tend to be high in fat, with the average accounting for 38% of total calorie intake. The main reason for high fat intake is that fats tend to give food an appealing flavor. For example, oil (100% fat) turns a bland potato into a delectable but nutritionally poor order of French fries and low-fat hamburgers never have that same flavor and mouthwatering taste as do their fat-laden counterparts. Some popular sources of fats include butter, salad dressings, fried foods, peanut butter, and baked goods such as cookies and cakes.

It has been well documented that the excess amount of fat in our diets is the primary nutritional cause for childhood and adult obesity. From an athlete's standpoint, fat-laden pregame meals serve no purpose in preparing athletes for aggressive competition. Fat is broken down much more poorly than carbohydrates during physical activity and therefore is a less efficient source of good nutrition for hockey players.

PROTEINS

Dietary protein is important for young athletes because it provides the building blocks for growing muscle and bone, and is necessary for repairing injured tissues. Protein has only a minor role in energy production. A normal North American diet has more than enough protein to fulfill these important functions. The main sources of dietary protein include meat, poultry, fish, eggs, and nuts.

Many athletes use amino acid or protein supplements in order to try to build greater muscle mass and improve performance. Unfortunately, these seemingly conscientious players are making not just one mistake, but two. Increased muscle strength is achieved with proper training that is specific to an athlete's sport. Increasing the amount of protein in a diet does nothing to stimulate additional strength gains. In fact, excess protein from dietary supplements is simply turned into fat for long-term storage and high levels of protein can place stress on the kidneys. Over time, this stress has the potential to cause permanent damage to the kidneys.

In the early 1980s, pregame meals for professional athletes generally consisted of a large sirloin steak, a baked potato with sour cream, vegetables, and then ice cream for dessert. My Edmonton Oilers teammates and I generally ate this meal before every road game and often when playing at home as well. Little did we know that this mouthwatering meal was, from a performance standpoint, as much a detriment as it was an advantage. The meal provided a good supply of dietary nutrients from all food groups; however, it was not conducive to producing the high level of energy required for the game. The steak, though a good source of protein, the building blocks for muscle, was unfortunately a negligible source of instant energy for a game six hours later. The baked potato and vegetables provided some calories from carbohydrates, but most of the players topped the potato with a good-sized helping of sour cream, a high-fat condiment. Ice cream was a tasty way to finish the pregame meal, but was unfortunately also high in fat.

In the late 1980s many teams, including the Oilers, began to examine pregame meal planning. As a result, spaghetti with tomato sauce served with salad and buns or bread became common fare. Looking back, it seems that the Oilers' first few Stanley Cup championships were won with hard work, talent, great team cohesion, camaraderie, and a lot of heart, but not with an optimal pregame dietary plan!

MINERALS

Minerals do not contribute energy to the body on their own but they are important for food metabolism and energy production. Certain minerals are important for maintaining muscle and body function. These include calcium, iron, sodium, potassium, zinc, and magnesium (iron and calcium are most commonly deficient in athletes). For competitive athletes, a well-balanced diet including all the food groups provides an ample supply of these minerals for good health and body function.

Minerals*

Mineral	Function	Source
Calcium	Is important for bone hardness, muscle contraction	milk, cheese, clams, broccoli, turnips
Chlorine	Maintains fluid balance in the body	table salt
Chromium	Regulates blood sugar levels	liver, cheese, whole grain cereals
Copper	Is involved in nerve structure	liver, shellfish, nuts, whole grain cereals
Fluoride	Decreases tooth decay	fluoridated water
Iodine	Is required by the thyroid gland	iodized salt, seafood
Iron	Is important for formation of red blood cells	liver, meats, egg yolks, dark green vegetables
Magnesium	Is a bone constituent	cereals, nuts, meats
Manganese	Is involved in enzyme activation	legumes, nuts, whole grain cereals
Molybdenum	Is an enzyme cofactor	meats, legumes, cereals
Phosphorous	Enhances bone structure	milk, cheese, eggs, fish, poultry
Potassium	Affects fluid balance and nerve irritability	fruits, vegetables, meat, fish, cereals
Selenium	Is an antioxidant	meat, seafood, cereals
Sodium	Affects body fluid balance	table salt, processed foods, milk, meat
Sulfur	Is a protein component	eggs, meat, fish, poultry, nuts, milk
Zinc	Is an enzyme constituent	seafood, liver, yeast, wheat germ

* This list is only a sample of the mineral functions and sources.

There are only two exceptions to this rule. Vegetarian athletes must be careful to ingest sufficient iron since sources of iron that are readily used by the body are found primarily in meat products. In addition, female athletes may require iron supplements due to regular monthly blood losses during menstruation. If there is a concern about any mineral requirements, then it is a good idea to consult with a family physician or a registered dietician for further advice.

The chart on the previous page contains a list of the main minerals, their functions, and food sources for each. This is not a complete list, but is a handy reference for coaches who wish to provide nutrition information to their players.

VITAMINS

Vitamins are important compounds that assist in producing energy for the working muscles. They are not a direct energy source like carbohydrates;

however, like minerals, vitamins are required to maintain a healthy body. There are two main types of vitamins:

1. *fat-soluble*
2. *water-soluble*

An excess of fat-soluble vitamins—A, D, E, and K— is stored in fatty tissues throughout the body. Water-soluble vitamins—B and C— on the other hand, have limited storage capacity in the body. If excessive amounts are ingested, then water-soluble vitamins are simply excreted from the body by the kidneys.

Vitamin supplements are almost always unnecessary for optimal performance by competitive hockey players. In almost every case properly balanced meals will provide sufficient amounts of the important vitamins without the need for supplementation. However, athletes who are strict vegetarians may be deficient in Vitamin B_{12}.

The chart below contains a list of the main vitamins, their functions, and food sources for each.

Vitamins*		
Vitamin	**Function**	**Source**
Fat Soluble Vitamins		
A	Maintains visual acuity	fish-liver oils, dark, leafy vegetables
D	Regulates calcium absorption	fortified milk, fish-liver oils, sunlight
E	Is an antioxidant	vegetable oils, nuts, green, leafy vegetables
K	Assists with blood clotting	liver, cabbage, spinach
Water Soluble Vitamins		
C	Aids formation of connective tissue	citrus fruits, melons, broccoli, potatoes
B_1 Thiamine	Is important for carbohydrate use	breads, cereals, meat, nuts
B_2 Riboflavin	Involved in energy production	milk, eggs, liver, green, leafy vegetables
B_3 Niacin	Releases stored energy	meat, poultry, fish, breads, nuts
B_6	Enhances protein metabolism	meat, fish, poultry, potatoes, vegetables
B_{12}	Aids red blood cell formation	animal foods only: fish, meat, eggs
Folic Acid	Aids red blood cell production	meats, cereals, fish, green, leafy vegetables

* This list is only a sample of the vitamin functions and sources.

THE TECHNICAL, THE PHYSICAL, AND THE MENTAL GAME

This is not a complete list, but it is a handy reference for coaches who wish to provide nutrition information to their players.

WATER

In the past, water was thought to play only a small part in the proper functioning of a well-conditioned body. However, many studies have shown that water is indeed a valuable component of energy production for competitive athletes. Since one of the byproducts of muscle usage during sports is heat, the body requires a mechanism to rid itself of the excess heat produced during exercise. Lacking this mechanism, an athlete would quickly become lethargic, weak, and unable to perform even simple physical tasks.

Nature, however, has provided us with sweat glands throughout the skin surface to allow for the release of heat.

> *…3% dehydration can cause a 10 to 15% decrease in power output in the body.*

When skating hard during a practice or a game, the body's sweat glands secrete water onto the skin's surface. As the water evaporates, the skin is cooled and generalized body overheating is prevented. There is only one problem with this effective form of self-cooling. If the body's water level is not replenished, then it can become dehydrated. In the past dehydration was not considered to be a big problem until studies began showing its devastating effects on performance. Studies have shown that as little as 3% dehydration can cause a 10 to 15% decrease in power output in the body. In practical terms this means that a 100-pound hockey player will be significantly fatigued due to dehydration alone after losing only three pounds from sweating during a game.

Since it is hard to control external factors such as arena temperature and intensity of play, it is important that players drink ample water before, during, and after practices and games. Some wait until they become thirsty to start drinking water. However, thirst should not be used to gauge the need for fluid intake because a person is already slightly dehydrated when he begins to feel thirsty.

As with most health conditions in our bodies, prevention is the best way to combat dehydration. Young players should be encouraged to drink water regularly during the season and especially during times when they have back-to-back games or practices. The best way to gauge adequate hydration is to check the color of urine. If it is dark and concentrated, then it is likely that the player is

During my career in the NHL, my playing weight was about 215 pounds. I played in several Stanley Cup series and when we advanced all the way to the finals, we often played into May. Our opponent in the final series was always a team from the east coast—the New York Islanders, the Philadelphia Flyers, or the Boston Bruins. By mid-May the temperature was blistering hot in these cities and the rink environment often reflected the outdoor conditions. During one particular game on Long Island, I weighed myself before and after the game. I started the first period at 215 pounds and after a bruising, end-to-end three periods of hockey I weighed in at 198—a 17-pound weight loss in two hours! This was, of course, almost exclusively water loss through sweating. That works out to be about 8% dehydration. Like many others, I thought I was exhausted at the end of the game because it was such a grueling match. Little did I know that my exhaustion was, for the most part, due to being significantly dehydrated! The amazing part of this story is that I drank regularly during games, taking a sip of water between almost every shift!

dehydrated and requires larger amounts of fluid. If, however, urine is dilute and faint in color, then the player is doing a good job of staying well hydrated. Therefore, to ensure adequate fluid intake, four cups (1 liter) of cool water should be consumed before activity, and an additional half-cup (125 mL) every 15 to 20 minutes.

Timing for a Pregame Meal

In the NHL, players enjoy the consistency of a regular routine on game day. In almost every case, teams playing at home have a pregame skate from 10:30 AM to 11:30 AM. Following practice the players generally go home and eat their pregame meal around 12:30 to 1:00 PM. On the road, teams practice between 11:30 AM and 12:30 PM, then return to the hotel for a meal at 1:30 PM. Most players are back in bed by 2:00 PM for a pregame nap and then wake up at 4:00 or 4:30 PM to begin mental preparations for the upcoming game. For both home and visiting teams the pregame meal is about six or seven hours before the first puck drops.

This same routine is, of course, impossible for minor hockey players who must go to school on weekdays or who have afternoon games on the weekends. For these players it is recommended that a pregame meal consisting primarily of carbohydrate-loaded foods be consumed not less than four hours before the start of a game. The timing allows the food to be properly digested so that the level of available sugars in the blood is increased prior to competition. It also allows for the gastro-colic reflex* to act. This reflex stimulates the large intestine once food has entered the stomach and is the reason why a bowel movement is often necessary immediately after a large meal. A hockey player who eats a meal shortly before beginning play may suffer abdominal cramping. Unfortunately, this condition can be detrimental to performance.

If a young hockey player has a game or practice midevening—at about 7:30 PM—a normal supper meal of high carbohydrate foods eaten at about 5:00 PM should be well

Running a 26-mile marathon is one of the most grueling challenges in the world of sports. Since these events last three to six hours for most participants and they generally are held on hot summer days, marathons are almost always started early in the morning to avoid midday heat. Because of the timing of the event, marathoners often eat a large carbohydrate meal the evening before. They then leave for the race immediately upon waking to begin their exhausting challenge. Often, runners "hit the wall" at about the 20-mile mark. This is due to the complete exhaustion of glycogen stores available to the working leg muscles. Glycogen is the storage compound for glucose and other sugars in the body that becomes readily available during longer athletic events. A recent study has shown that marathoners who do not eat a small snack on the morning of an event may have a significant decrease in muscle glycogen levels compared to someone who has eaten a nutritious breakfast! Applying this research to hockey, it is apparent that a snack before those early morning practices or games is not just a good idea; it is a necessity!

---

* gastro-colic reflex—the body's response to food entering the stomach that causes increased contractions of the large colon, initiating the urge to have a bowel movement

absorbed and not cause stomach discomfort during play. For a game at 6:00 PM, only one hour after supper, a player may be wise to consider a snack,

such as a piece of fruit or sandwich, before leaving home and then have a more substantial meal after the game. If players must practice very early on the weekends, then it is not prudent to have a large breakfast before stepping onto the ice. It is, however, essential that they have some sort of nutrition prior to leaving for the rink. A banana, a muffin, or a glass of juice is an easy way to fulfill an athlete's nutritional requirements for early morning play.

Considering the recommendation that a pregame meal should be about four hours before game time, there is an apparent discrepancy in the National Hockey League's routine of meals six hours prior to a game. It may be that the professional players are simply accustomed to this routine, even if it is not as physiologically sound as eating a meal later in the day. Some teams have begun the practice of providing muffin, juice, and fruit snacks to players at 5:00 or 5:30 PM immediately prior to boarding the bus for the arena in the hope of ensuring optimal nutrition for the game.

Postgame Nutrition Strategies

Even though a minor hockey game lasts only one to two hours, the energy reserves in a young player's body will likely be somewhat depleted. Research involving long distance runners has shown that following activity, it is beneficial to consume foods that are high in carbohydrates in order to restore glycogen levels, an important compound for future energy needs. A milkshake and an order of French fries may not be the best postgame meal choice, since the high fat levels of these foods stimulate energy replenishment in the form of fat deposition to a much higher degree.

It is recommended that parents and coaches encourage young players to try juice, fruit, pasta, or bread-filled postgame snacks in order to refill the body's energy stores for the next game. Some teams even raise additional funds in order to offer juice or a piece of fruit to players after each game so that every player gains this important performance advantage!

A Final Word about Nutrition & Hydration

- Try to eat a regular pregame meal no less than four hours before game time.

- If four hours is impossible, then eat only a carbohydrate-filled snack.

- Avoid protein, amino acid, and other supplements; they can be dangerous.

- Drink water at regular intervals during games and daily to prevent dehydration.

THE TECHNICAL, THE PHYSICAL, AND THE MENTAL GAME

- Avoid ingesting excess food as this can lead to obesity and poor performance.

- Eat postgame snacks such as fruit, muffins, juice.

- Avoid fast food even though it is convenient because it is usually high in fat.

The days of nutritional ignorance when it comes to athletics are soon to be gone. Coaches are well advised to discuss good nutrition with their young charges regularly. Once is not enough! It is important for young athletes to have a good understanding of the kind of foods that can enhance their performance. A high carbohydrate, low fat diet with lots of fluids is a combination that will enhance the performance of athletes of all ages.

5 - Stretching, Warmup, & Cooldown

For many young hockey players, the excitement of the game begins when they first put skates to ice. Getting to the rink, dressing, and the pregame talks are usually thought of as the routine to "endure" in order to experience the thrill of new hockey challenges. Similarly, these players think proper stretching and warmup are insignificant aspects of a player's preparation for a game. On the contrary, it is important for coaches to encourage players to think about stretching, warming up, and cooling down as integral parts of preparation for any game or practice.

This chapter includes a discussion on the importance of stretching, types of stretches, technique, information on warming up before a game and cooling down afterwards, and a whole body stretching program that players can use before games or practices. The Appendix to this book contains practice plans that include warmups, stretching, and cooldowns.

Why Stretch?

There are two main reasons why it is important for young hockey players to stretch before a practice or a game. First, stretching helps to decrease the incidence of joint or muscle strains during high intensity activity. It is widely agreed that slowly taking a muscle to its optimal length prior to competition reduces the

chance of a muscle pull and also increases flexibility across the adjacent joints, thereby protecting them as well. A strong and limber biceps muscle, for instance, helps to protect the elbow joint from injury and at the same time makes it more efficient during use.

Second, a regular stretching program gives an athlete the chance to relax mentally before games. This kind of preparation is beginning to be recognized as valuable for players of all ages. It allows the player to prepare mentally before a game and to clear distracting or non-hockey concerns from his mind in order to focus on the game to come.

...a good warmup routine increases the blood flow to the working muscles, preparing them for peak performance.

In a sport that involves aggressive skating movements, a good warmup routine increases the blood flow to the working muscles, thereby preparing them for peak performance. Consequently, a routine that includes both stretching and warmup should be an important part of a regular pregame preparation.

Types of Stretching

There are two general categories of stretching techniques:

1. static and ballistic
2. passive and active

STATIC AND BALLISTIC STRETCHING

Static stretching is the most common and safest form. It involves gradually stretching a muscle to its farthest point and then holding it there for a recommended 10 to 20 seconds. The slow stretch of the muscle to its maximum length not

Static Stretch

only helps to prevent muscle pulls but also allows for optimum performance when increased demands are placed on the muscles during a game. The 10 to 20 second hold will maintain healthy muscle length and should be encouraged at all levels.

Ballistic stretching is characterized by rhythmic bouncing and bobbing motions. This type of stretching is potentially dangerous if done improperly. Bending over quickly to touch the toes is an example of a ballistic stretch: it also happens to be a good way to pull a muscle! Ballistic stretching, therefore, is not recommended for athletic preparation.

Ballistic Stretch

PASSIVE AND ACTIVE STRETCHING

Passive stretching is a paired stretching technique where one person manipulates a limb or the body of a teammate into a stretched position while that person keeps his muscles completely loose. This technique has been widely used in the past but unfortunately has a greater potential for injury than active stretching and is therefore discouraged for young players.

Passive Stretch

Active stretching is where players use their own muscles to perform the exercise. This slow, sustained stretch of a muscle to its maximum length is accomplished by athletes moving their own joints. Bending over while keeping the knees straight is an example of an active stretch for the hamstring muscles of the legs. Compare this with a passive stretch, where another person pushes the athlete farther over to increase the stretching distance.

Active Stretch

On the whole, active/static stretching is by far the best technique of stretching for skating athletes because the benefits to the working muscles are greater and the risk of injury is reduced.

Stretching Technique

It is important to know the proper technique for stretching, but it is just as important to understand the role of specific muscles during skating in order to be adequately prepared for the stresses placed on them during a game. Breathing should be normal and regular during the stretch, with the emphasis on breathing out when moving deeper into the stretch. The most important thing to remember is not to force a stretch beyond a muscle's normal range. Players must be patient and work their way slowly into a more intense stretch.

Before a game or practice it is common to see players step onto the ice, skate to a corner, and  proceed to sit or lie down to do their stretching routine. This is detrimental in two important ways. One of the reasons for stretching before a game or practice is to warm up the muscles. The last thing a player should do is lie down on a large pack of frozen water. That is more likely to cause the body and muscle temperature to drop. It is far better to perform pregame stretching drills in the dressing room and, if the dressing rooms are too small, then out in the lobby. Players can also do a good set of stretches before leaving home for the rink. On-ice stretching also seems to be a waste of valuable ice time—time that could be better spent practicing skating, agility, passing, or other hockey skills.

Many experts now recommend a dynamic stretching and warmup routine that includes sitting or prone stretches done off-ice and stretching maneuvers for the back, legs, and arms done while skating around the perimeter of the rink. It is thought that stationary off-ice static stretching combined with a dynamic on-ice, active stretch routine, where players are actively skating while stretching their muscles, prepares the body's muscles more effectively to perform at optimum levels and also reduces the risk of serious injury.

Hockey Warmup

Many skaters do not warm up before a practice or game. By leaving this step out, they significantly increase their chances for injury because they have not properly prepared their muscles for activity. A warmup should be designed in such a way as to prepare the body for higher intensity exercise. Blood flow and muscle temperature increase, and joints loosen up in preparation for intense activity. The increased muscle temperature not only helps to prevent injuries; it also enhances the performance of those muscles. We start a car in the winter to allow the engine and the lubricants to warm up so that the working parts will perform as they are intended to. The same is true for our bodies.

To warm up:

1. Begin with a whole body exercise to raise the heart rate above resting levels— a light jog or bicycle ride for at least two minutes.

2. Follow with joint flexibility exercises. Focus on active, static stretching of the muscles that will be involved in the activity or game.

Exercise the whole body.

Gradually increase intensity.

3. Increase exercise intensity gradually at the start of a practice or game. Take the first few laps around the rink slowly, focusing on extending the skating stride fully.

4. Shortly thereafter, try higher speed sprints and agility turns to both sides.

At the end of a warmup that includes these elements, a player's muscles should be well prepared for aggressive hockey competition.

Hockey Cooldown

Try higher speed sprints.

Intense exercise causes the body to produce a waste material called lactate in the working muscles, therefore, in order to return to the ice refreshed and ready to perform at a high intensity for the next game, athletes must work to rid their muscles of these wastes. Performing cooldown routines helps speed the rate of recovery from a workout and also helps return the body to the normal rested state. Thus, it is important to gradually lower exercise intensity at the end of a workout in order to slowly decrease heart rate and blood pressure. Then follow the cooldown activity with some flexibility exercises.

To cool down:

1. Begin the cooldown with a half-speed skate around the rink at the conclusion of practice. This allows the muscles to more efficiently recover for the next game and is better for the muscles than doing full-speed sprints then directly leaving the ice and sitting down in the dressing room.

2. Do a simple routine of active, static stretching exercises following a practice or game in order to assist in recovery and to maintain muscle length and flexibility.

In reality, young players recover so easily from physical exertion that the notion of a cooldown is not so much for enhanced muscle recovery as it is establishing pre- and postgame routines that will become much more important as they mature. If good habits are started early, then they are often followed through life!

Hockey Stretching Program

For skating sports, there are many excellent stretches that players can perform before every practice and game. However, it is important to select stretches that a coach feels comfortable with and that prepare all the muscle groups used in skating. It makes sense to follow a routine that begins with the feet and works all the way up to the head. It is an effective way to remember the stretches for each muscle and each part of the body.

> *...follow a routine that begins with the feet and works all the way up to the head.*

Following is a group of ten stretches that work each of the major muscle groups used in hockey. This group of stretches begins at the feet and continues up the body for a whole body warmup. The Appendix includes sample practice plans that include warmup, stretching, and cooldown routines.

STRETCH #1—ANKLES

1. Sit upright in a chair or on the floor with one leg crossed over the opposite knee as shown.

2. Hold just above your ankle with one hand.

3. Grasp the toe portion of your foot with your other hand.

4. Exhale and slowly rotate the foot in a circular direction.

5. Continue rotating in both directions for 10 to 20 seconds.

6. Relax.

7. Repeat with the other foot.

STRETCH #2—CALF MUSCLES

1. Stand upright 2 or 3 steps from a wall.

2. Bend one knee and keep the other leg straight.

3. Lean against the wall without losing the straight line of head, neck, spine, pelvis, outstretched leg, and ankle.

4. Keep the heel of your straight leg down, flat on the floor and parallel to your hips.

5. Exhale and bend your arms, and move your chest toward the wall shifting your weight forward.

6. Hold the stretch for 10 to 20 seconds.

7. Relax.

8. Repeat with the other leg.

STRETCH #3—HAMSTRING MUSCLES

1. Sit upright on a table or bench with one leg extended out in front.

2. Keeping the left leg straight, exhale and bend at the waist, moving your upper torso forward. Make sure that the back stays straight during the stretch to prevent possible back strain.

3. Hold the stretch for 10 to 20 seconds.

4. Relax.

5. Repeat 2 or 3 times before switching legs.

STRETCH #4—GROIN A

1. Sit upright on the floor with your legs flexed and heels touching each other.

2. Grasp your ankles and pull them in as close to your buttocks as possible.

3. Exhale and lean forward from the hips keeping your back straight, and try to lower your chest to the floor.

4. Hold the stretch for 10 to 20 seconds.

5. Relax.

6. Repeat 2 or 3 times.

STRETCH #5—GROIN B

1. Kneel on all fours with the toes pointing backwards.
2. Keep the arms straight with the hands on the floor.
3. Exhale and slowly spread your knees apart trying to lower your hips to the floor.

4. Hold the stretch for 10 to 20 seconds.
5. Relax. This is one of the most deceptively intense stretches for the adductor (groin) muscles.

6. Repeat 2 or 3 times.

STRETCH #6—QUADRICEPS OR THIGH MUSCLE

1. Stand upright with the legs together.

2. Bend one knee and hold the foot close to the buttock with the hand on the same side.
3. Hold onto a wall or chair with the opposite hand to keep your balance.
4. Keep the back straight and knee pointed straight down.
5. Hold the stretch for 10 to 20 seconds.
6. Relax.
7. Repeat with the other leg.

STRETCH #7—HIP FLEXOR MUSCLES

1. Kneel down on one knee with the other bent to 90° and your foot flat on the floor.

2. Keeping the lead foot flat on the floor, slowly move the hips forward.

3. Keep your back straight and feel a stretch in the front of the rear hip.

4. Hold the stretch for 10 to 20 seconds.

5. Relax.

6. Repeat with the other leg.

STRETCH #8—ABDOMINAL MUSCLES

1. Lie face down on the floor with body extended.

2. Place your palms on the floor beside your hips with fingers pointing forward and elbows slightly bent.

3. Exhale and slowly press down on the floor, raising the head and the trunk, and arching the back. Feel the stretch across the abdominal muscles.

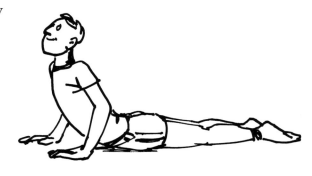

4. Hold the stretch for 10 to 20 seconds.

5. Relax.

6. Repeat 2 or 3 times.

THE TECHNICAL, THE PHYSICAL, AND THE MENTAL GAME

STRETCH #9—TRUNK MUSCLES

1. Stand straight up in an open area.

2. Grasp a hockey stick with both hands and rest it across the shoulders.

3. Exhale and turn your upper body to one side as far as possible.

4. Hold the stretch for 10 to 20 seconds.

5. Relax.

6. Exhale. Return to the starting position and turn your body the opposite direction.

7. Repeat 2 or 3 times in each direction

STRETCH #10—SHOULDER MUSCLES

1. Sit or stand upright with one arm raised to shoulder height.

2. Flex one arm across to the opposite shoulder.

3. Grasp the raised elbow with the opposite hand.

4. Exhale and pull the elbow across the chest.

5. Hold the stretch for 10 to 20 seconds.

6. Relax.

7. Repeat with the other arm.

A Final Word about Stretching, Warmup, & Cooldown

Few young hockey players take heed when they are
told that stretching and warmup help to prevent
injuries and that a proper cooldown helps to prepare
muscles for the next workout. However, if they are
told that stretching can help them to develop a faster
shot, become a better skater, and be stronger in front
of the net, then all may be more receptive. During
the formative years of a player's life, developing a
positive attitude towards proper stretching and
warmup is an important step that all coaches should
convey to their young athletes.

Chapter 5

6 – Equipment Fitting & Maintenance

Over the last twenty years, the quality of hockey equipment has greatly improved, providing more protection to amateur and professional hockey players than ever before. Sporting goods stores across the country have ample selection and knowledge-able staff who can assist parents and players with the purchase of helmets, sticks, gloves, skates, and pads. However, players and parents should consider two main aspects of hockey equipment when making purchases: proper fit and adequate maintenance.

1990s 1950s

Proper Fit

If properly maintained, then hockey equipment should last for many years, usually far longer than a player can fit into it. Many urban centers have used equipment outlets where parents can trade in older equipment that is too small. These outlets provide an effective solution to the major concern facing families when it comes to hockey equipment, that is, getting a proper fit without exorbitant cost.

Hockey registration has become so expensive that, in order to keep costs to a minimum, some parents

purchase helmets, sticks and skates larger than required so that they will last more than one season. In most cases this economic strategy simply makes it more difficult for young players to develop their hockey skills. A stick that is too long is more difficult to use for stickhandling or passing drills. Skates that are two sizes too large often make it impossible to maneuver easily and learning to skate can become a more difficult chore.

THE HELMET

> *Wearing an improperly sized helmet is dangerous...*

While some pieces of oversized equipment simply make playing the game difficult or inconvenient, there is one piece of equipment that when sized improperly becomes a hazard to the player—the helmet. Wearing an improperly sized helmet is dangerous because it increases the chance of serious head injury when players come in contact with the boards or other players.

To fit a helmet correctly, follow these steps:

1. Have the player put on the helmet.
2. Secure all the straps.
3. Grasp both sides of the helmet and try to rotate the helmet without also rotating the head.

4. Look for any looseness or extra helmet movement.

5. If you are at all unsure of the fit, request assistance from knowledgeable sporting goods staff.

Coaches should check the fit of all players' helmets in this way before the beginning of the season's first practice and at regular intervals throughout the season. A shoulder bruise or knee ligament sprain seriously affects no one's life but an improperly fitting helmet can mean a life-altering or life-threatening head injury. Prevention is the only way to protect our children from this danger.

THE STICK

On any hockey bench there is often a vast array of stick lengths. Though much of the variation is due to different player heights, it is also necessary when sizing a stick to consider the player's skating style. The general rule of having the stick extend up to the chin or nose when a young player stands up straight is a good place to begin. As players develop their skills, however, some will feel more comfortable skating in a more upright position while others will skate more efficiently with their hips bent and chests closer to the ice. Upright skaters usually prefer longer sticks that have a higher lie.*

---

* The lie of the stick is the angle between the blade of the stick and the shaft. On a stick with a higher lie the shaft extends more vertically when the blade is flat on the ice.

When I played I used a Lie 6 stick because I tended to skate in a more upright fashion. Unfortunately, this skating style also made me a rather slow skater, as I did not develop an effective bent knee position during my stride. On the other hand, former teammate Wayne Gretzky had a more bent-over skating style. It was a position that allowed him to be agile as well as quick to snag loose pucks. His trademark stick was about a Lie 4 and almost as long as mine was even though I am much taller. Somehow he could maneuver so gracefully with the puck using a stick that the rest of us could hardly handle. When I hear a young player complaining about a stick, I think back to Wayne's puckhandling magic using a stick that many would ridicule. However, he often scored three or four points every game and the opposition certainly wasn't laughing!

GLOVES AND PADS

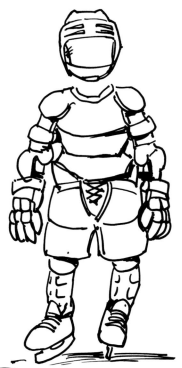

There is a vast selection of hockey pads and gloves that can be purchased at sporting goods stores. Although personal preference is a consideration, an important rule for properly fitting equipment is that there should be no exposed areas of the body that could be subject to injury. Elbow pads should be long enough to extend from the bottom of the shoulder pads all the way to the top of the player's hockey gloves. Shoulder pads must be large enough to cover all the vulnerable bony areas on a player's body; glove cuffs long enough, and finger shafts fitted to the player's hand. If this is not the case, then the player is at higher risk of injury to an area unprotected by equipment. On the other hand, equipment cannot be so large that it impedes skating and fluid body movement.

Maintenance: Drying and Storage

One of the great aspects of the game is its intensity of play. With that hard work comes overheated young bodies and sweat—moisture and odor—that permeates the air of dressing rooms and a player's equipment. In order to preserve the quality and function of a player's equipment, players must have a maintenance routine when they remove their equipment. If equipment is left sopping wet with perspiration in a hockey bag for several days, then the protective shells and inner liners break down more quickly and require earlier replacement.

It is worthwhile for parents to consider allocating a special area at home that can be used for hanging equipment to dry after every practice and game. This area may be in the garage or basement, but it should be kept separate from other non-hockey items so that equipment is not misplaced or forgotten. Drying out hockey equipment regularly not only extends its life but also allows parents, coaches, and players to enter a slightly less offensive dressing room after workouts!

A Simple Equipment Rule

Every year most teams are faced with a familiar dilemma. A player loses or forgets a glove, helmet, or other piece of equipment. This situation usually presents itself just before the start of a game or practice. The result is that coaches and parents scramble for replacement equipment, borrowing from other players or racing home to pick up the missing piece.

Players must understand that they are responsible for their own equipment. A bit more time taken by coaches and parents at the beginning of each season will help to avoid similar incidents. Teaching hockey beginners the following simple equipment rule will stand them in good stead during their entire hockey careers. This simple procedure, if used regularly, will prevent those uncomfortable and frantic scenes that seem to occur in hockey rinks across the country.

EQUIPMENT RULE

Once dressed for a game or practice, players should stuff their hockey bags under their benches in the dressing room. This provides an uncluttered area for coaches who wish to give a pregame or prepractice talk. It also allows players to exit the dressing room more easily. Once the practice or game is over, players then pull out their bags and open them. As they undress, each piece of equipment is put directly in the bag. If players are conscientious about such a routine, then it is virtually impossible to misplace a glove, shin pad, or any other important piece of hockey gear.

After drying the equipment at home, it is equally important to ensure that each piece of equipment is put back in the bag in preparation for the next game or practice. Players who are taught this rule and who habitually practice it will not have sit on the bench during a game while someone searches for the missing article.

A Final Word about Equipment

In a contact game like hockey the quality of the protective equipment, equipment fit, and proper maintenance should never be overlooked. These protective components make the difference between a player suffering a serious injury or playing unhurt for the rest of the season. In addition, although the cost of participating in hockey continues to rise, the advent of used equipment stores allows all children to enjoy this great game regardless of financial background.

7 - Hockey Injuries

Hockey is a fast-paced sport full of physical contact and emotion. It is not a sport for the weak or fainthearted yet people of all ages, abilities, strengths, and weaknesses can enjoy it. It is important for all those involved in hockey—coaches, managers, parents, and players—to have some understanding of the injuries that can happen during a practice or a game. Reading this chapter will by no means qualify a person to diagnose, treat, and rehabilitate hockey-related injuries. However, it will provide some insight into why injuries happen, what to look for, and how to react when one occurs.

I have never considered myself a true scholar—it may have had something to do with all the concussions I suffered playing hockey! In any case, I like to keep things simple when it comes to remembering injuries that occur in the body. The description of injuries begins at the top with head and neck injuries, proceeds down the body, and concludes with maladies of the ankle and foot.

> *...coaches of every team must have an Emergency Action Plan in place...*

Before injuries happen, though, coaches of every team must have an **Emergency Action Plan** in place so that when injuries do occur on the ice, the coach and any assistants know exactly what to do.

Emergency Action Plan

Have you ever been to a hockey game when a player is hit from behind and rammed headfirst into the boards, and then crumples in a heap to the ice? Have you ever been the coach who is responsible for assessing that same situation? Have you ever been the parent of the injured child wondering frantically what should be done to ensure proper care for your son or daughter? Every hockey parent and coach at one time or another has thought about situations like this, yet few have taken proper steps to be prepared for on-ice emergencies.

A valuable first step in being prepared for a serious on-ice injury is certification in first aid and CPR. I

recommend that at least one coach on every team be certified in both first aid and CPR so that informed decisions and a treatment plan can be initiated following any type of injury. Many hockey associations, including the Canadian Hockey Association, require that at least one bench coach on every minor hockey team take a hockey trainers course. This course provides information to team management and coaching staff on preventing and preparing for various hockey injuries as well as on risk management issues.

Developing an **Emergency Action Plan (EAP)** is the most important way to prepare for a serious on-ice injury. The plan outlines specific responsibilities for people associated with the team in case a player sustains a serious head or neck injury. There are three main people involved in carrying out an Emergency Action Plan:

1. *Charge Person*
2. *Call Person*
3. *Control Person*

The duties and responsibilities of these important people are described below.

CHARGE PERSON

The charge person is the individual who goes immediately to the assistance of an injured player. He or she should be the most qualified individual in first aid and CPR training on the coaching staff.

The charge person must:

Charge Person

- reach the injured player safely, usually with the assistance of another player or referee.

- ask the injured player a question to determine if he is conscious. If the player is unconscious, then put the Emergency Action Plan in motion.

- ask the conscious player if there is any neck pain, if he or she can move arms and legs, or if there is any numbness in the arms or legs. If there is neck pain or numbness, then it may be a serious injury, such as a fractured neck vertebrae or broken neck. This condition can be worsened by aggressively moving the player. Before moving the player, therefore, the charge person must be absolutely certain that there is no injury to the player's neck. If there is pain in the neck, paralysis, or numbness in the arms or legs, then put the EAP in motion.

- after verifying that the neck is not injured, slowly begin the process of carefully moving the player off-ice. At least two players or referees should help, as it is difficult and slippery to walk on the ice wearing street shoes. Refer to specific injury sections for hints about assisting players with other nonemergent injuries. However, if there is any hint of a neck or head injury, then let caution be your guide and put the Emergency Action Plan in motion!

- accompany the player to the dressing room for further evaluation of the injury and possible transfer to the nearest emergency department or physician's office.

If the Emergency Action Plan is put into action, then the charge person must:

- ensure that the player is not moved at all.
- immobilize the player's neck by firmly placing hands and forearms on either side of the player's head without moving it. The charge person should choose a relatively comfortable position when immobilizing the player's neck because he may have to stay in that secured position until the ambulance attendants arrive.

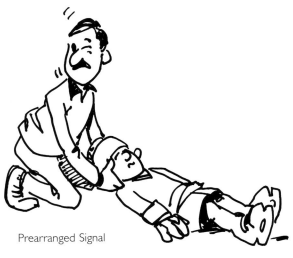
Prearranged Signal

  - have a prearranged signal with the call person to indicate that help is required and to make a call for an ambulance.
  - not allow the player's head, neck, or body to move until experienced ambulance personnel arrive at the scene, assess the situation, and take over care of the player.

- monitor the player's breathing if unconscious.
- accompany the injured player to the hospital and provide comfort and reassurance to the player as well as pertinent medical information and details of the injury to the hospital medical staff.

CALL PERSON

The call person is typically the manager of the team. He or she is someone who sits in the stands during the game and regularly attends games.

The call person must:

> Immediate treatment of a player who is neither breathing nor has a pulse is beyond the scope of this book. For more information about these situations, refer to available CPR manuals.

- know the location of a working telephone that can be used in case of an emergency.

- know the correct emergency telephone number for the area where the arena is located and, if a pay phone must be used, then have sufficient coins.

- know the best route to the arena and the most appropriate entrance for the emergency personnel to use, considering ease of stretcher use and ice surface access. In the case of double or quad arenas, it is crucial for the call person to be aware of the correct ice surface where the game or practice is being held.

- report back to the charge person once the emergency call has been made and report the estimated time of arrival of the ambulance.

Call Person

- go to the appropriate emergency access area of the arena and wait for the ambulance.

- direct emergency personnel to the proper location in the building.

CONTROL PERSON

The control person is typically an assistant coach who is on the bench at the time of the injury. Upon seeing that the Emergency Action Plan has been initiated, the control person should

- enter the ice surface safely and approach the site of injury.

Control Person

- disperse the crowd that usually congregates around an injured player. An injured player is usually in pain. Well-meaning but inexperienced teammates and parents huddled closely around can make the player feel worse.

- after dispersing the crowd, wait for instructions on relaying information to the injured player's parents if one or both are present in the arena. There is no more helpless feeling than seeing your child lying on the ice and not knowing the extent of the injuries.

- be available for any physical assistance that the emergency personnel may require while transporting the injured player out of the building.

The Emergency Action Plan is an absolute requirement for hockey teams at all levels. As the name states, it is a well-organized plan of action that is implemented in the case of a serious injury. The three individuals involved should practice and discuss the EAP regularly.

...practice and discuss the EAP regularly...

The scene of a serious head or neck injury is not the time or place to try to remember what must be done and by whom. Few situations like this occur in hockey; however, any instance where lack of preparation causes more serious injury or death is one too many! Awareness and preparation are essential!

The Appendix to this book contains a condensed version of the Emergency Action Plan. This may be photocopied for quick reference.

> *"If I had six hours to chop down a tree, I'd spend the first four hours sharpening the axe."*
> *–Abraham Lincoln*

Head and Neck Injuries

The one injury all coaches must be familiar with is a serious neck injury. Broken bones mend and torn ligaments heal but an injury resulting in a player becoming a paraplegic is a devastating injury and a situation that all coaches must try to prevent. There are seven vertebrae in the neck held together by ligaments and soft tissue, making the neck particularly vulnerable to serious injury.

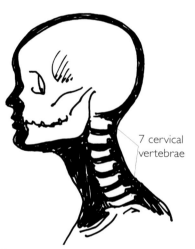

7 cervical vertebrae

With continuing improvements in the design of helmets and face shields and an increase in their use, the incidence of head and face injuries in hockey has dropped drastically. However, it remains important for coaches and parents to ensure that players of all ages use properly fitting, approved helmets and face shields every season.

PREVENTION

Education is the single most effective way to prevent serious head or neck injuries. It is possible to teach young players to play hockey safely without diminishing the aggressive aspect of the game. The majority of serious head and neck injuries occur near the boards, where contact with this immovable barrier is the result of a collision or body check. It is vital to teach players early on to receive passes near

the boards with their backs to the boards and their eyes scanning for the puck as well as for any other players in the vicinity. I often say to my team "Bums on the boards!" Players soon realize that they can receive a pass more easily in this position. Also it is virtually impossible to sustain a serious head or neck injury since any contact with the boards is made with a less vulnerable part of the body. If coaches emphasize this technique at every opportunity during practice sessions, then players soon perform it automatically.

Because of increased protection from improved equipment, many players now carry their sticks much higher and tend to play more recklessly. Referees must take the responsibility to penalize players and coaches must discipline players who carry their sticks high or hit from behind. A policy of zero tolerance for this kind of play will also aid in preventing head and neck injuries.

WHEN AN INJURY OCCURS

Only qualified people (medical personnel or trained Emergency Response Teams) should move players with suspected neck injuries.

It is important to follow the flow of the game and to watch how and where accidents occur. When a player collides headfirst with the boards or lands awkwardly with a bending force to the neck, carry out the following steps to protect against further injury:

1. Assume that a neck injury has occurred.

2. Get down beside the player and ask the player if he or she is hurt.

3. If there is no response, then the player is unconscious and has suffered a third degree concussion. Begin your **Emergency Action Plan** (see pages 143–149).

4. If the player is conscious, then ask if he or she has any pain in the neck area or elsewhere.

5. If the player has any pain in the neck or has numbness or tingling in any limb, then begin your **Emergency Action Plan**.

> *Do not move a player who is unconscious or who has any neck pain.*

Do not move a player who is unconscious or who has any neck pain. This is very important. Unfortunately, there have been cases where a player with a fractured spine has been improperly moved and serious spinal cord injury has resulted.

The other neck injury that must be considered is a deep cut to the soft tissues around the neck area. Since the jugular vein and other important blood vessels are located relatively close to the skin, it is possible for a skate blade to cut deeply enough to cause profuse bleeding. Proper treatment of a deep cut anywhere on the body but especially on the neck is direct pressure on the cut with a clean towel or piece of cloth and proper assessment as to whether the Emergency Action Plan should be implemented.

RECOGNIZING AND DEALING WITH AN INJURY

Types of Concussions

A concussion is simply defined as a temporary disturbance of neurological (nervous system) function caused by trauma (head injury). The most commonly identified concussion occurs when a player is knocked unconscious. This is called a third degree concussion—the most dangerous and potentially the most serious head injury. With a second degree concussion, the player experiences no loss of consciousness but suffers from post-concussive systems (confusion, dizziness, blurry vision, or impaired concentration) for more than 15 minutes. A first degree concussion is when a player does not lose consciousness and has complete resolution of any concussive symptoms in less than 15 minutes. Fewer than 10% of concussions result in loss of consciousness

A player may have a concussion and not lose consciousness.

Recovery from a Concussion

With concussions of all degrees it is vital that a player completely recover from the injury for a specific period of time before resuming play. There are several sets of guidelines that describe the conditions for safe return to activity following a concussion. Although there is no consensus within the medical community about which are the most appropriate, the American Academy of Neurology Guidelines (as shown on the opposite page) are the ones most recently proposed.

Concussions—Symptoms & Recovery

Types of Concussions	Indicators	Recovery Time
First Degree	no loss of consciousness	symptom* free in 15 minutes
Second Degree	no loss of consciousness	symptoms* for longer than 15 minutes
Third Degree	loss of consciousness	

Guidelines for Return to Play**

First Degree Concussion	Return to play after 20 minutes with no symptoms. The Canadian Hockey Association recommends that any player suffering a first degree concussion should be seen by a physician before returning to play. After a second first degree concussion, no play is allowed for one week after all symptoms have cleared both at rest and with activity. After three first degree concussions in one season it is recommended that players discontinue active participation in a contact sport for the remainder of the season.
Second Degree Concussion	Return to play after being symptom-free for one week. After two second degree concussions, return to play after two weeks symptom-free. Discontinue active participation after three second degree concussions in one season.
Third Degree Concussion	Return to play after being symptom free for two full weeks. After two third degree concussions in one season, return to active participation after being symptom free for four weeks. Discontinue active participation after three third degree concussions in one season.

* Post-Concussive Symptoms: dizziness, headache, confusion, blurred vision, nausea, poor concentration, memory changes

**Guidelines of the American Academy of Neurology

Doctors have become much stricter about players returning to a contact sport while still feeling the effects of a concussion. This is because of the rare, but dangerous, **Second Impact Syndrome** (SIS) that can occur in athletes who return to contact sports while still experiencing symptoms from a concussion of any degree. With SIS the result of even a gentle hit can be rapid swelling of the brain which, in virtually all cases, causes death. Although SIS is rare, it is critical to ensure that a player who has had a concussion is fully recovered before being allowed back on the ice! It is vital that parents, coaches, and managers, in consultation with doctors, make the final decision on when to return a player to competition. In most cases the player would return as quickly as possible without the considering the potentially serious consequences. There is no room for error when it comes to head injuries!

A helmet is only protective if it fits properly.

PROTECTION

To test for proper helmet fit, have the player put on the helmet. Grasp it with both hands and try to move it about the head. A properly fitted helmet will not move around on the player's head when rotated or when trying to lift it directly off the player's head. For step-by-step instructions on checking helmet fit, refer to Chapter 6, "Equipment Fitting and Maintenance."

Though a neck guard may be a nuisance to wear, it can be a lifesaver.

The neck has several important blood vessels located directly under the skin including the jugular veins that carry blood directly from the head to the heart. Because there is no protection for these veins, such as the ribs which protect the heart, a cut from a skate blade can have devastating consequences.

Consequently, for players of all ages, neck guards must be considered compulsory equipment. No person regardless of his or her medical background looks forward to treating a lacerated jugular vein in the middle of a hockey rink!

Shoulder Injuries

The shoulder is the most common site of a hockey injury because it is usually the first part of the body to make contact with immovable objects like the ice surface and the rink boards or moveable but solid objects like goal nets and other skaters. Most players suffer an injury to the shoulder at least once during a hockey career. Therefore, it is important to be aware of types of shoulder injuries that can occur, their severity, and the proper forms of rehabilitation required so that players can return to play as quickly as possible.

PREVENTION

Techniques for giving and receiving checks are skills that develop slowly in young players. Less experienced players often place themselves in compromising positions on the ice where they may not see an opposing player approaching to make a check. By becoming more adept and aware, a player is more likely to position himself with head up and be fully aware of the location of the puck and other players close by. Maintaining a "heads up" aware position certainly helps to prevent shoulder injuries.

Some players feel that dropping a shoulder down before a collision increases power to their hits. Unfortunately, this hitting technique also leaves the shoulder vulnerable to a shoulder separation. It is important to teach young players to keep their shoulders level when they make body contact with opposing skaters. Not only does this position help them to keep their heads up, but they are also more likely to come out of the collision injury free!

WHEN AN INJURY OCCURS

It is usually obvious when a severe shoulder injury occurs. Spectators, parents, and coaches recognize the direct contact made and notice a player favoring one arm. Occasionally the injury is severe enough that the player is unable to leave the ice without assistance. It is essential that the person who is assisting the injured athlete does not yank on the affected arm, because even more damage may result.

Unlike head and neck injuries, shoulder injuries are not potentially life threatening, so once it is determined that the site of injury is the shoulder, help the player to the dressing room for further evaluation. If in intense pain, then the player should see a physician immediately. If, however, the pain is manageable, then a qualified trainer or manager can remove the player's jersey and shoulder pads for a closer look.

RECOGNIZING AND DEALING WITH AN INJURY

There are three main types of shoulder injuries, all involving different parts of the shoulder and caused by various mechanisms. These are

1. *fractured clavicle*
2. *separated shoulder*
3. *dislocated shoulder*

Fractured Clavicle

A fractured clavicle—a broken collarbone—typically occurs in two ways.

- A player is hit directly over the top of his shoulder with the stick of another player. The direct pressure of such a blow can break the small, S-shaped bone (the collarbone) that lies quite close to the skin at the top of the shoulder.

- A player is hit into the boards shoulder first. The compressive forces of such a hit can break the clavicle, usually in its weakest area—between the inner third and outer two-thirds of the bone.

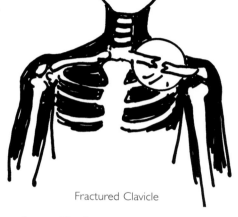

Fractured Clavicle

A player with a broken collarbone feels obvious pain and extreme tenderness directly on the collarbone area. Any movement of the shoulder is painful. Although very painful, a fractured clavicle on its own is not a medical emergency unless accompanied by arm pain or numbness on the same side as the fracture. The player can be transported to the doctor's office or emergency department by car. It is important that coaches and parents become aware that the high cost of an ambulance trip is unnecessary for injuries that are accurately assessed on site as being nonemergent.

It is often said that if a person must have a broken bone, then it should be the collarbone, because it heals so well. Players with fractured clavicles are often put in a figure-of-eight splint to decrease the discomfort and to keep the bone in proper alignment while it mends. Healing of the collarbone usually takes six weeks; however, players are generally restricted from returning to contact hockey for at least eight weeks because of the chance of rebreaking the clavicle with another forceful hit. Before returning to play, player, parent, and coach should check the shoulder pads for proper fit and ample protection to the area over the clavicles.

Separated Shoulder

A separated shoulder is by far the most common shoulder injury in hockey. It usually occurs when a player is hit shoulder-first into the boards, a goal post, or another player. There is a strong ligament near the corner of the shoulder that stabilizes the AC joint (acromio-clavicular joint), holding two of the shoulder bones together. A shoulder separation occurs when these bones are hit with sufficient force causing the ligament to be stretched or torn. There are three general grades of shoulder separations:

• **First Degree AC Separation**. With this mild injury the player has pain when direct pressure is applied to the top of the shoulder area at the AC joint. There is usually minimal swelling or bone abnormality. A first degree AC separation injury requires no therapy and is usually completely resolved with seven to ten days of rest. It is important that the player stay away from further contact during the recovery period so that a minor first degree separation does not accidentally become a second or third degree injury!

• **Second Degree AC Separation**. With this more severe injury, there is still tenderness on the crown of the shoulder. Pulling down on the arm may cause a small step or widening between the bones forming the AC joint area on the injured shoulder whereas there is no change on the unaffected shoulder when the arm is pulled. When a physician takes x-rays the player may be asked to hold weights for half the x-rays. This is done to see if the joint comes apart with traction, revealing the injury to be a second degree separation. A second degree separation typically takes four to six weeks to heal completely. The player requires aggressive therapy, regular ice treatments, and no physical contact until completely pain free.

• **Third Degree** AC **Joint Separation.** This most serious of separations is easy to diagnose because the end of the collarbone protrudes much more than on the uninjured side. Even though the shoulder appears to be quite deformed, a third degree separation does not typically require surgery. After four to six weeks of therapy, the player will have a good functioning shoulder in almost all cases. If the shoulder has full range of motion and strength, and there is no pain, then the player is safe to resume playing

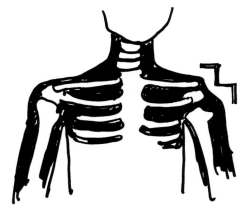

Step Deformity of a 3rd Degree
AC Joint Separation

hockey. The collarbone may continue to protrude more prominently that the uninjured side, but it is only a cosmetic concern. Nearly every NHL dressing room has at least one player who demonstrates the remnants of a third degree shoulder separation.

Dislocated Shoulder

A dislocated shoulder is the most damaging and most painful of all shoulder injuries. It is also the shoulder injury that can cause the most long-term problems. The

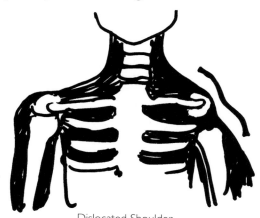

Dislocated Shoulder

Just three weeks prior to the start of the Stanley Cup playoffs, I dislocated my left shoulder after stepping on the blade of a broken hockey stick. My shoulder rotated outward and back when I hit the ice. I sensed immediately that I had dislocated my shoulder. Off to the hospital I went. The surgeon quickly popped my shoulder back into place. Although it generally takes at least six weeks to recover from an injury of this type, I was back in the lineup for Game One of the playoffs. So much for proper and complete rehabilitation when it comes to the Stanley Cup playoffs! Fortunately, I have had no long-term problems with my shoulder. However, returning from an injury too early should never be recommended for any amateur player.

shoulder joint is rather shallow. The ball and socket of the joint stay in position with the help of numerous strong muscles and ligaments. Occasionally, as a result of a body check or a hit into the boards, a player's shoulder will be wrenched backwards and outward causing the ball of the arm bone (humerus) to come out of its socket. A skilled trainer or a physician may be able to retract the arm and put the joint back into place. This maneuver may not be particularly difficult; however, it should be performed by an experienced health care professional.

The real concern with a shoulder dislocation is that it tends to recur, and if it recurs regularly, then surgery may be necessary to tighten the shoulder joint. Nearly every physician has seen an athlete who has recurring shoulder dislocations, to the point where any movement causes the ball of the joint to pop out of its socket. This situation is preventable and surgery is typically recommended once a dislocation has occurred more than two or three times. Restricted activity, ice, and therapy with aggressive strengthening of the shoulder muscles are the recommended treatment for dislocations.

PROTECTION

In almost all cases of shoulder injuries in hockey, there is contact made between the shoulder and a solid object. Therefore, it is crucial that players have properly fitting protective shoulder pads to minimize the risk of injury. Years ago shoulder pads were nothing more than leather-covered felt strapped over each shoulder to afford some protection from injury. As the speed of the game increased and the focus on body contact heightened, cantilever-style shoulder pads were developed to spread the compressive forces more evenly across the entire shoulder. The larger rigid shoulder cup no longer rests directly on the point of the shoulder, but rather sits above it in a levered design. With this style of equipment it is now much less likely that contact with a stick, the boards, or another player will cause damage to the underlying shoulder.

Arm and Hand Injuries

Playing the game of hockey requires the ongoing use of hand and arm motion to control the hockey stick during play. Because of this, injuries to the arm or hand can make playing difficult. All too often these injuries are ignored because they are not considered serious. As a result many eventually turn into chronic problems that can last the entire season or longer.

PREVENTION

Proper protective equipment is vital to the prevention of injuries to the arms and hands. However, just as important is the ability of a player to maintain good positioning on the ice and not be caught in an awkward stance during contact. Bruised elbows, jammed wrists, and sprained thumbs often occur when players are not aware of the play around them and, as a result, they are not prepared for contact with other players or the boards. Good positioning technique and a 360° awareness of the play is the first and most important step in preventing arm and hand injuries.

WHEN AN INJURY OCCURS

Most serious injuries to the arms and hands are easily noticeable. An angulated forearm suggests a broken bone, and a finger that is pointing in an odd direction likely indicates a dislocation. Except for simple bruises to the muscles of the forearm, injuries to the arm and hand should be immobilized using a simple sling or splint and the player should be transported to a hospital or clinic for medical evaluation. X-rays are often required to rule out serious problems. Treatment may include casting or surgery and rehabilitation is specific to the injury sustained.

RECOGNIZING AND DEALING WITH AN INJURY

Arm Injuries

Arm and hand injuries are divided into two basic groups—traumatic and overuse. Due to the physical nature of the game of hockey, traumatic injuries to the arms occur regularly. Players are often slashed across the forearm or elbow by an opponent's stick, causing a significant amount of pain. Bones are seldom broken when injured in this way; however, swelling and bruising in the relatively tight forearm area can produce ongoing discomfort for many days. Overuse arm injuries, on the other hand, are caused by repetitive forces that cause strain or discomfort on one part of the body. Unfortunately, overuse injuries may become chronic if not resolved when they are first noticed.

Two common arm injuries associated with hockey are:

1. *Bursitis*
2. *Lateral Epicondylitis (tennis elbow)*

- **Bursitis** (a traumatic injury). Occasionally, after a body check or simply during skating, a player falls directly onto the ice hitting an elbow. There is a small sac of fluid called a **bursa** located directly over the elbow bone. If the bursa is hit with enough force, then it can become swollen and red. This swelling is sometimes described as a "goose egg," but the correct name is bursitis. If large enough or inflamed, elbow bursitis can prevent further play even with proper elbow protection because it becomes too painful to bend. Treatment may include ice, therapy, and even draining of the bursa sac by a physician using a syringe and needle.

- **Lateral Epicondylitis** (an overuse injury). The arm that is used to hold the upper end of a hockey stick requires sufficient strength to maneuver the stick in the air and to control the puck, often when the other hand is not holding on. There are several muscles in the forearm that straighten the wrist, and many attach on the outer part of the elbow. If a hockey player overuses these muscles while stickhandling, then the muscles can get inflamed and sore. The resulting condition is called **lateral epicondylitis**, commonly called "tennis elbow." This is another injury that can put a player on the bench until the pain is completely resolved. Ice and therapy are often good for early treatment of this injury as it sometimes becomes a chronic problem.

Hand Injuries

Many hand injuries can occur in a physical game such as hockey, but there are five that are common enough to warrant discussion. They are:

1. *Carpal Ligament Sprain*
2. *Scaphoid Fracture*
3. *Ulnar Collateral Ligament Sprain*
4. *Broken Finger*
5. *Boxer's Fracture*

- **Carpal Ligament Sprain.** The wrist is made up of eight small bones, all of which are connected by strong ropelike connective tissue called ligaments. It is quite common for a hockey player to have a hand jammed directly into the boards or twisted while checking another player. Considerable pain may result and even though x-rays show no broken bones, this type of injury can cause ongoing discomfort—often until the end of the season. A professional player with this kind of wrist injury often has the wrist taped every game and practice so that he can continue to play. Because ligaments have a relatively poor blood supply as compared with muscle, they tend to heal quite slowly. As a result sprained carpal ligaments can become chronically painful if continually re-aggravated. Aggressive therapy is often required to completely rehabilitate this injury.

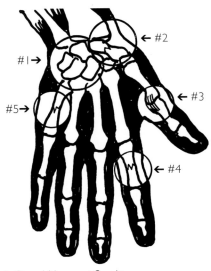

1. Carpal Ligament Sprain
2. Scaphoid Fracture
3. Ulnar Collateral Ligament
4. Broken Finger
5. Boxer's Fracture

- **Scaphoid Fracture**. One of the eight wrist bones is called the **scaphoid bone** and is located at the base of the thumb. The scaphoid is often injured when a hockey player jams a hand into the boards or when his stick is levered with a twisting motion during contact. The bone is quite long and thin and, unfortunately, following an injury, x-rays often do not show a fracture even if one is present. Because of this, many doctors will cast the wrist despite a normal x-ray if they suspect a broken scaphoid. Since the bone receives its blood supply from only one end of the bone, there can sometimes be incomplete healing which results in ongoing pain and disability. In fact, players who have suffered scaphoid fractures occasionally must undergo bone grafting of the site just to ensure proper healing. For this reason, a physician should evaluate any pain at the base of the thumb following a jarring injury.

- **Ulnar Collateral Ligament Sprain**. Slightly farther down the thumb from the scaphoid is a ligament called the **ulnar collateral ligament**. Though it is small, this ligament is very important in providing stability to the thumb as well as providing the strength to grip a hockey stick. A twisting injury to the thumb can stretch or completely tear this ligament. The result is often significant swelling and pain. Unlike most bruises, however, if this ligament is completely torn, then the thumb will never regain full function unless surgery is performed to stabilize it. This injury is often called "skiers' thumb," because, like players holding hockey sticks, skiers often experience a severe twist of a ski pole during a fall that puts a great force on the base of the thumb. A physician should see any thumb injury that does not resolve in three or four days in case therapy or a referral to a plastic surgeon is required.

During the 1988 Winter Olympic Games in Calgary, we were playing Team France. A defenseman slashed at me on a power play and caught the end of my left little finger. I knew instantly that the bone was cracked, but with a little tape and the adrenaline from playing in the Olympic Games, I was back playing before the period was over. It is interesting that, although I remain pain-free to this day, when the weather changes I still get an annoying numbness at the end of that same finger!

- **Broken Finger**. It is not uncommon for a hockey player to be slashed accidentally across the glove while handling the puck. Occasionally an opponent's stick hits an unprotected part of a finger. The bone at the end of the finger can be cracked or broken. This can be an especially painful injury, especially if blood begins to collect under the fingernail. X-rays should be taken depending on the severity of the pain and often a finger splint is used for immobilization.

- **Boxer's Fracture**. A player who drops his gloves to fight often lands a punch with the hand in a crooked position, breaking the outer part of the hand. This fracture of the fifth metacarpal bone, or so-called "boxer's fracture," is quite common in older age groups and often occurs when an angry player punches a door or wall in frustration, which leads to more frustration as well as a broken hand! Occasionally these fractures have to be set if they are angled too much, but most simply require a cast for four weeks.

PROTECTION

Properly fitting elbow pads that do not rotate or slide down the arm are the most effective weapons against elbow injuries. Young players should not wear elbow pads that are too large because they inhibit the ability to stickhandle. Conversely, pads that are too small leave protection gaps on the forearms which then become prime targets for errant slashes.

The length of the fingers in hockey gloves is important because finger holes that are too short put players at high risk for bruised and broken fingers. The cuff size of the glove is also significant as it provides valuable protection to an area frequently hit by opposition sticks during checking. Many NHL players are using shorter cuffed gloves to allow for better ease in stickhandling. Unfortunately, they are also giving up valuable protective padding, leaving the wrist more vulnerable to some of the injuries listed in this section. Well-fitting shoulder pads, elbow pads, and gloves should leave little unprotected space along the entire length of the arm. For more information on proper fitting of gloves, see Chapter 6, "Equipment Fitting and Maintenance."

Back Injuries

Injuries to the lower back are common in hockey because of the bent-over style of skating. In addition, body contact and collisions with the boards often cause twisting forces applied to the back, which result in ongoing discomfort. Identifying and treating back injuries early is vital so that a hockey player with back pain can return to play as soon as possible after treatment.

PREVENTION

In many levels of hockey, September tryouts are often the first time that players lace up their skates since the previous spring's playoffs. Although most players stay active during the summer by playing baseball, soccer, or other sports, none of these activities simulate the bent-over position that is required for optimum skating performance in hockey. A significant increase in stress on the lower back over a short period of time is often the cause of early season back pain. Fortunately, with proper planning and slow progression from off-season activities to regular skating, most early season back pain can be avoided.

Most experts suggest that high resistance weight training should be delayed until a young player reaches physical maturity at about age sixteen. However, younger players can work at keeping their abdominal and back muscles strong and flexible. A simple strength-training program is an excellent way for players to prevent the repetitive stresses of skating from turning into a chronic back injury. Most athletic trainers who work with hockey players implement a core strengthening program as part of their overall fitness training. A variety of back and abdominal exercises can be done by players of all ages to help prevent overuse back pain.

WHEN AN INJURY OCCURS

It is rare for a mid-ice check or a collision with the boards to cause a serious lower back injury where the player loses feeling and strength in his or her legs. However, if a player has these symptoms even for a few seconds, follow your Emergency Action Plan (see pages 143–149). An ambulance and trained personnel should transport the player to the nearest hospital.

More commonly with back injuries in hockey, the muscles supporting the low back are strained and go into spasm. This usually takes a few hours and most players find that they are quite stiff the next morning. Applying ice to the low back is an excellent initial treatment for back spasms, usually applied for 20 to 30 minutes every hour. Back pain that lasts for more than a few days may require some form of active therapy for complete resolution of pain.

> *Do not move a player who experiences loss of feeling or numbness in his legs or lower back.*

RECOGNIZING AND DEALING WITH AN INJURY

A player who experiences a back injury involving loss of feeling or strength in the legs must be moved using a spine board with immobilization. X-ray investigation at a hospital is mandatory for these rare but serious injuries. More commonly, however, a player comes off the ice feeling a slight twinge in the lower back, following a hit or a play along the boards. The player may be able to continue skating, but often the back muscles stiffen up and the player must be removed from the game. Early application of ice is one good way to decrease the pain and stiffness that will occur in the lower back area. A good rule of thumb to follow is that if back pain lasts for longer than three or four days, then the player should consult a physician.

There is one other type of back problem that commonly affects young male hockey players, but it is not due to any contact during a game. There is a

My wife, Kathy, was a two-time Olympic speed skater for Canada. She would often train in Germany during the winter with the National Team. She remembers not so fondly the first two or three weeks of every season enduring the aching lower back pain that almost all the skaters suffered. Although they were in fabulous condition aerobically, it still took time before they became accustomed to the daily three or four hours of skating that stressed their lower backs. By the time the Olympics or World Championships were held, all the skaters had their back muscles fully prepared for the stress of such a physically demanding and exciting sport.

condition called **spondylolisthesis** that occurs when a section of the lower back vertebrae becomes unstable and one of the vertebra slips forward on the one below. This condition occurs in up to 4% of all young children and the onset can be insidious. Although in most cases the problem is benign, occasionally it can progress and eventually require surgery to stabilize the lower back. For this reason, a physician should examine a player with lower back pain that tends to persist throughout the season. Early identification and aggressive abdominal and back exercises are often all that is needed to allow these players to continue to play pain free.

PROTECTION

Every joint in the body has two requirements in order to stay healthy and function properly—flexibility and strength. To protect hockey players from lower back pain, an off-season routine of exercises designed to strengthen the muscles surrounding the joints and to increase flexibility is an effective way to keep players skating all season and away from the ice packs! A complete series of dryland strength and flexibility exercises are beyond the scope of this book. Refer to *Hockey Drill Solutions*, another book in the *LifeSport* series.

Hip and Groin Injuries

In any sport where there are solid barriers used to define the field of play and physical contact is a legal component, injuries to bones close to the skin naturally occur. The hip area is one where direct contact with the boards or the ice can cause painful injuries.

By observing the way that the lower limb moves during the skating stride, it is no surprise that groin injuries are common. Not only is early identification of a groin injury important, but proper and full treatment is also vital to ensure prompt return to pain-free skating.

PREVENTION

In almost every instance in hockey, a direct blow to one of two bony prominences on the outside of the hip joint causes hip injuries. Consequently, prevention of hip injuries involves protecting these vulnerable areas with sufficient padding. Groin injuries, on the other hand, are generally caused by extreme forces on the muscles of the inside of the legs, either because of a slip or from forceful contraction of the muscles during a skating stride. Like other muscles used in sport, it is imperative that groin muscles are strong, flexible, and properly warmed up to ensure optimal performance as well as to prevent injury.

WHEN AN INJURY OCCURS

Following a hit into the boards where the hip bone is injured, a player is often in too much pain to skate off the ice. Once a coach or trainer identifies the injured area as the hip and has determined that there are no associated head or neck injuries, then the player can be assisted off the ice for further assessment in the dressing room.

Most groin pain, however, tends to progress slowly and the player often continues to play until the muscle stiffens. The player may only become aware of the pain after the game when the groin muscles cool off and begin to tighten.

As with most soft tissue (muscle) injuries, the recommended early treatment for both hip and groin injuries is the **RICE** principle:

R—Rest
I—Ice
C—Compression
E—Elevation

1. **R = Rest**—Restrict any physical activity that aggravates the pain.

2. **I = Ice**—Apply an ice pack to the area for 20 to 30 minutes at least twice daily.

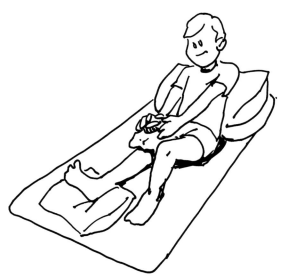

3. **C = Compression**—Wrap the injured area firmly both during and between icing sessions to maximize the effectiveness of the treatment and to minimize swelling.

4. **E = Elevation**—For lower extremities, keep the leg above the level of the heart to allow gravity to help reduce swelling.

RECOGNIZING AND DEALING WITH AN INJURY

Recognizing Hip Injuries

It is quite rare for the thick and well-muscled hip bone to be fractured from direct contact with the hockey boards or following a fall on the ice. However, a bone bruise on the outer aspect of the hip, called a hip pointer, commonly occurs. Usually insufficient protective padding in the hockey pants is the main cause of a hip pointer injury, but quite often even good quality but poorly fitting pants can allow for too much movement during wear, thus causing the unprotected hipbone to be frequently exposed.

There are two main areas where the hip can be injured:

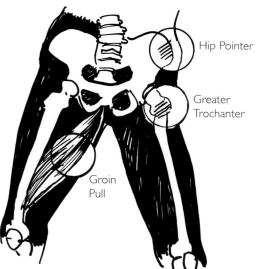

1. the iliac crest
2. the greater trochanter

- **The Iliac Crests**. The iliac crests are located at the top of the pelvis and are bony ridges that can easily be felt on either side just below the waistline. An injury to this area is called a "hip pointer" and a bruise in the area is usually very painful since there is little soft tissue between the skin and the hip bone. Because there are many nerve fibers on the outer covering of a bone, the **periosteum**, a bone bruise on the iliac crest can be quite debilitating. Interestingly, players who use rigid belts to hold up their hockey pants are often at greater risk of getting a hip pointer. The belt is usually tightened just above the edge of the hip bones and because the belt is fastened snugly around the body, there is often little padding underneath to prevent a hip pointer.

- **The Greater Trochanters**. Located slightly below the iliac crests at the top of the legs, these are actually part of the thighbone. The greater trochanters are bony ridges on the outside part of the upper thighs that can also be injured by direct contact. Between this bone and the overlying skin there is a fluid filled sac called a **bursa**. A blow to or friction over the trochanteric bursa results in swelling and inflammation that is known as **trochanteric bursitis**. Because this area of the hip is stressed regularly when skating, players suffering from this type of injury have difficulty skating.

Treatment of Hip Injuries

Immediate treatment for hip pointer bruises and trochanter bursitis should include icing the area in order to relieve pain and reduce swelling. Therapy can also speed relief and recovery. Treatments such as ultrasound and interferential current aid in accelerating pain relief and recovery. Ultrasonic waves are believed to help to increase blood circulation to promote tissue healing. Interferential current is primarily used to reduce pain and also promotes faster recovery. Strengthening exercises are important to ensure that the hip area does not weaken following the injury. Stretching is also important to ensure that the muscles retain their normal length. It is vital that players regain full range of motion, flexibility, and strength before returning to play or they may risk reinjury. An experienced therapist can supervise these components of rehabilitation until there is complete recovery from the injury.

Recognizing Groin Injuries

Groin injuries occur in two basic ways:

- An explosive movement or change in direction puts a great deal of stress on the groin muscles. If the muscles are either stiff or too weak to handle the stress, small muscle fibers can tear, causing a muscle strain.

- The other way a groin injury occurs commonly affects goalies when they stretch out to make a pad save. Unfortunately they may stretch a little farther than the muscle is prepared to go, again causing a muscle injury.

Unlike a traumatic hip pointer, a groin strain may not be severe enough to cause the player to leave the ice. Unfortunately, further injury may occur before the player realizes the severity of the initial strain.

Treatment of Groin Injuries

Proper treatment includes the application of ice and compression to the affected muscle area. It is also necessary to restrict the player from skating at full speed until fully rehabilitated. Proper therapy including ice, ultrasound, muscle stretching, and strengthening programs are vital for early return to play pain free.

Coaches and parents in consultation with doctors or therapists must agree that a player has full range of motion in the injured groin muscle, full strength, and no pain when striding hard using the muscle before returning to full-speed skating. If not, then he is likely to reinjure the same muscle and possibly be doomed to play for the rest of the season with an aching, chronic groin injury!

PROTECTION

Like almost all muscle injuries in hockey, prevention comes down to two major factors— proper protective equipment and a good warmup/stretching program. Hockey pants, like every other piece of hockey equipment, must fit properly, be in good condition, and have padding that protects the vulnerable areas of the hip. In addition, although most players believe that playing the game is the most important part of hockey, a good stretch and warmup is essential so that the game can be enjoyable and injury-free! For more information on fitting protective equipment refer to Chapter 6, "Equipment Fitting and Maintenance."

It is important for coaches of young players to encourage their players to develop good stretching and warmup habits. Although it is unlikely that a young eight- or ten-year-old will pull a groin while skating, it is a good idea to start them off early so that regular stretching becomes an automatic part of their lifelong hockey experience.

Knee Injuries

One of the most common sites of injury in any sport is the knee, and hockey is no exception. Because a serious knee injury has the potential to end a hockey player's career, it is most important for coaches, parents, managers, and the players to fully understand the nature and severity of any knee injury.

PREVENTION

Long before a bag of ice is taped onto an injured knee, take steps to minimize the occurrence of injuries. Most knee injuries occur in two ways.

- Direct contact with another object may cause a twisting force to the knee. The object can be an opponent's knee, a goal post, or the rink boards. Improved skating agility, muscle strength, flexibility, and endurance as well as careful positional play are some of the strategies that can be used to prevent this type of contact injury.

- Accidentally catching a skate blade in a rut may cause a player to suffer a torquing force on the knee or ankle of the affected leg. It is important for arena staff and coaches to ensure that the quality of ice surface is monitored so that these unusual but potentially devastating injuries are prevented.

WHEN AN INJURY OCCURS

Although a knee injury is not life threatening, appropriate early treatment can minimize its severity. If coaches and managers follow the flow of the game, then they can often identify the way a player is injured. When an injury occurs that may be knee related, follow these steps:

1. If an injured player cannot skate off the ice under his own power, then the trainer or manager should first determine whether a head or neck injury has occurred.

2. Once it is established that the site of the injury is the knee, then the player should be removed from the ice as quickly as possible.

3. One or two adults should then help the player off the ice, being cautious until completely off the ice surface.

4. Apply ice to the knee immediately after the injury. This is the proper and normally the only treatment that should be carried out by the coaching staff or manager. Apply an ice pack or a half-full bag of snow directly to the knee and hold it securely in place with a compression wrap. If the knee injury appears to be serious, then transport the player immediately to a local emergency department or medical center. It is better to be safe than sorry!

RECOGNIZING AND DEALING WITH AN INJURY

Although there exists the potential for dozens of knee injuries, three main classes of injuries tend to occur. These include:

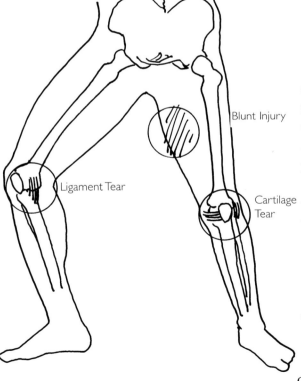

1. *blunt injuries*
2. *ligament sprains*
3. *cartilage tears*

Being aware of how an injury occurs is of great assistance when determining the type and severity of the problem. With information related to how the injury occurred, a physician will often know the type of knee injury that a player has sustained even before looking at the knee. The history of the injury is valuable to a physician and an alert coach or manager can relay information regarding the mechanism of injury that the physician would not otherwise have.

Blunt Injuries

These knee injuries happen frequently in hockey, where a sliding or off-balance player bangs a knee directly into an immovable or solid object, like a goalpost or the boards. This accident can result in a minor bruise—an ice pack and rest may be all that is required. If the force is more significant, however, the cartilage under the kneecap may be injured, resulting in a sore joint that is painful to bend. Kneecap (patellar) injuries may or may not swell, but they are extremely painful and occasionally require several months to fully heal. Finally, severe direct forces to the knee can result in either cracked or broken bones in the joint. In case of cracked or broken bones, swelling usually occurs immediately. The player is in extreme pain and is unable to move the injured knee. Transportation by stretcher and immediate evaluation at a hospital is the best solution in this case.

Quite often the blunt force does not hit the knee itself, but rather the thigh muscle above the knee. Typically, a quadriceps contusion or "charley horse" occurs as the result of illegal knee to thigh contact or a mid-ice hip check. Since these injuries are so common and frequent in hockey, many people believe that they are rather innocuous and often undertake little or no treatment. With a "charley horse," however, there is bleeding into the muscle tissue in the front of the leg. It usually takes from two to ten days for the bleeding to eventually be reabsorbed into the system at which time the knee regains full mobility. Unfortunately, if a player returns to play too early, before the muscle has completely healed, a serious problem can occur. A repeated hit to the same area of the leg can cause further bleeding often leading to a calcium buildup

In my medical practice, I saw two unfortunate young hockey players with myositis ossificans in a two-week span. The unusual twist was that I saw both players in July while they were playing summer hockey! Apparently, due to the rather short summer hockey schedule, both of these players tried to get back to playing before they were fully healed and paid dearly for that bad decision. This is an indication that even in the off season it is important for players to ensure they are completely healed before returning to competition.

in the thigh muscle. This condition, called **myositis ossificans**, may lead to long term disability and may require surgery to remove the calcium deposits from the leg. This potentially debilitating injury is almost totally prevented by ensuring proper and full rehabilitation before the injured player resumes contact drills and games.

Ligament Sprains

The knee is a major component of the lower limb and it requires strength, speed of movement, and stability in order to function properly. The knee joint is stabilized by several strong muscles in the thigh and calf that are used to bend and straighten it during skating. For strength, strong ropelike structures called ligaments are present throughout the knee joint and allow bending and straightening movement to take place without the knee giving way.

Because of the structure of the knee, the most common injury to the knee is a sprain or partial tear of the ligament, called the **medial collateral ligament (MCL)**, that is located on the inside of the knee. If a player is hit from the outside of the knee while his skate is firmly planted on the ice, the strong force often tears the medial collateral ligament. The degree of tearing determines both the severity of the injury and the length of time a player will be out of the lineup. See the chart on the next page for details.

Another important ligament in the knee is the **anterior cruciate ligament**, located with the **posterior cruciate ligament** between the thigh and shinbones. These structures provide valuable stability to the knee because they prevent the knee from rotating and hyperextending during a forceful leg movement.

Although injured more commonly in sports like downhill skiing, soccer, and rugby, a serious cruciate ligament injury often does occur on a hockey rink. This injury is recognizable by an almost immediate swelling in the knee, as early as two to five minutes after the abnormal movement occurred. The player is usually unable to bear weight on or to move the injured knee. Sprained cruciate ligaments require active therapy to ensure proper healing and to minimize loss of leg muscle strength. A completely torn ligament requires surgery but, luckily, the newer arthroscopic surgery techniques provide excellent results in the vast majority of patients.

Ligament Injuries

Degree of MCL Injury	Pain	Injury to Ligament	Out of the Lineup
1	+	painful; minimal looseness	7–10 days
2	+++	painful; moderate looseness	4–6 weeks
3	++*	severe looseness	6–8 weeks

* Often a complete tear of the medial collateral ligament is not as painful as a partial tear because when the ligament is completely torn, there is no tension remaining on any of the fibers. Therefore, the pain is often less than when there are some intact ligament fibers such as in a second degree sprain.

In 1987, I was playing with Canada's Olympic Hockey Team just months before the Winter Olympics in Calgary. We were training in Grindewald, Switzerland. During a one-on-one drill behind the net, I collided awkwardly with another teammate. I vividly remember the feeling in my knee as it twisted during the fall to the ice. I could tell from the location and severity of the pain and the fact that I could not straighten the knee that I had likely suffered a torn cartilage. I was flown back to Calgary the next day, had surgery in less than twenty-four hours, and was back skating with the team three days after the surgery!

Cartilage Tear

Finally, almost everyone has heard of a friend, a relative, or a high profile athlete who has torn the cartilage in a knee. These cartilages are located around the outer edges of the joint. They act as shock absorbers for the knee as we walk, jog, or skate. With any unusual twisting force the cartilage may be sheared between the shin and thighbones, and a tear can result. The player feels pain immediately but, unlike a cruciate ligament injury, swelling usually takes several hours to develop. A player with a torn cartilage can often carry on with daily tasks such as walking and sitting, but knee pain increases significantly when he or she is asked to run, pivot, or skate at high speed. Cartilage injuries are rare in children under the age of sixteen, presumably because cartilage is more pliable in younger people and resists twisting forces better than in older athletes. Unfortunately, the inner two-thirds of the cartilage has minimal blood supply; therefore it does not heal on its own in most cases. Minor arthroscopic surgery is often required to either repair the torn cartilage or to take out the torn piece.

PROTECTION

It is almost impossible to provide enough equipment protection to the knee to prevent many of these injuries and still allow the player to skate at a reasonable speed. It is much more important for hockey players to keep their thigh muscles strong during the rigorous hockey season. The quadriceps muscle on the front of the thigh is the primary stabilizing force for the knee joint. That is why any dryland training program for young hockey players should include strength training for the thighs.

Secondly, young players must be taught to keep their heads up and be aware of their surroundings while skating. Many injuries that I see daily in our clinic could have been prevented simply by improved positional and ice awareness. The importance of this preventative measure cannot be stressed enough with young players.

Finally, as in other areas of sport, it is critical that coaches, managers, parents, and, most importantly, players understand the need to follow the rules of the game as set forth by the amateur hockey organizations. Players of all ages should be able to look forward to an enjoyable and pain-free hockey experience without the looming threat of a serious and potentially career-ending knee injury.

Ankle and Foot Injuries

Unlike sports such as basketball and volleyball where there is considerable rotation of the ankle and foot during play, the skating motion is typically a fluid one-dimensional movement that puts little stress on ankles and feet. However, there are a few injuries that can cause problems for hockey players at all levels.

PREVENTION

Even though the ankle and foot are securely protected in a rigid skate boot, the following considerations will help prevent foot and ankle injuries. Proper boot fit is imperative to adequately protect the foot from direct injury by pucks, sticks, and other skates.

The toe cup of the skate must be stable enough to withstand direct forces from high-speed pucks, with space between the toes and the end of the boot to help prevent direct injuries to the toes. The padded front covering of the skate boot (called the tongue) must extend high enough to overlap the lower end of the shin pads, thus providing continuous protection for the front of the shin. The shin area is vulnerable to being struck by a blocked shot or pass. Too often players try to get an extra year of use out of shin pads that are too short, which puts them at risk of a painfully bruised shin. In addition, it is common to see two or three players at every NHL training camp suffering from sore feet simply because of poorly broken in or poorly fitting skates. Extra time taken to purchase properly fitting skates saves players a lot of pain early in the skating season.

It is also important for coaches and managers to be aware of the quality of ice before players begin to skate. Catching a skate blade in a rut in the ice can cause a serious ankle injury. The resultant twisting of an ankle causes pain and swelling. Ensuring proper ice conditions is an effective way of helping to prevent ankle injuries in hockey.

WHEN AN INJURY OCCURS

As with most injuries to the extremities, treat foot and ankle pain initially with the RICE formula. In the case of the ankle, compression is important because the area tends to swell considerably and rehabilitation is often delayed simply due to the time required to reduce the swelling.

> *R—Rest*
> *I—Ice*
> *C—Compression*
> *E—Elevation*

Following a sprain of an ankle, apply ice immediately and use a tensor bandage to compress the ice around the most tender area. Many trainers even use felt pads that fit closely around the bottom of each ankle bone to reduce fluid accumulation in the soft tissue area.

Frequently parents and coaches wonder about the necessity of an x-ray following an ankle injury in order to rule out a bone fracture. Unfortunately the vast majority of ankle x-rays are a waste of health care dollars, since injuries most frequently affect the soft tissues and ligaments of the ankle. Doctors usually do not use x-rays for an ankle injury unless one of two conditions is present:

- The person is unable to bear any weight on the affected ankle.
- Pain is present when pushing on the back part of either ankle bone.

If either of these conditions is present, then a player may indeed have broken an ankle and x-ray investigation is needed.

RECOGNIZING AND DEALING WITH AN INJURY

One of the most important ways to recognize an ankle injury is to follow the flow of the game and identify the mechanism of injury. Typically an ankle injury is caused either by catching a skate blade in a rut or by a player twisting an ankle while falling to the ice after a collision. Managers and trainers should be suspicious of an ankle injury even before they reach the injured player on the ice if they have been watching the flow of play. Once an associated head or neck injury is ruled out, the player can be removed from the ice with assistance for further evaluation in the dressing room. Immediate icing and an assessment as to whether a fracture has occurred are appropriate at this stage. Referral to an emergency department or medical clinic may be required, especially if either of the two conditions stated in the previous section is present.

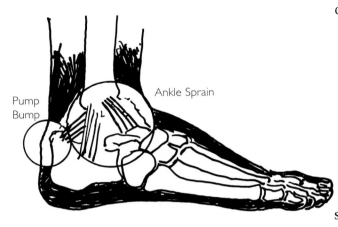

Pump Bump

Ankle Sprain

Two common hockey-related ankle injuries are:

1. *Ankle Sprain*
2. *"Pump Bump"*

Ankle Sprain

In the past, it was thought that an ankle injury was not serious and that to rehabilitate, simple rest was the treatment of choice. More recently physicians have realized that only half of this statement is true. Ankle sprains are certainly not life threatening; however, an active approach to rehabilitation is the optimal way to return these players to full skating form as soon as possible. It has been shown that in most cases, delayed or inadequate healing of an ankle sprain is the result of incomplete rehabilitation. Following a sprain, it can be worthwhile seeing a therapist who can instruct an injured player in a program that will return the ankle to full function. The program should include strengthening and stretching exercises, as well as a series of movements designed to help regain balance and to retrain the ankle muscles to full function.

"Pump Bump"

Foot injuries commonly present as pain over prominent bones, either in the heel area or throughout the toes. Properly fitting skates with appropriate width in the toe cap can usually alleviate toe discomfort; however, heel pain is often more challenging to manage. Located on the upper, outer part of the heel bone is a bony prominence that can become quite sore if continually rubbed by a poorly fitting skate boot. The bony ridge is called a **Hagelund's Deformity** or "pump bump" and it is more prominent in some athletes than others. Young players often come into a medical office with complaints of intense pain directly on the heel area so severe that they are usually unable to wear their skates at all. Although it is quite uncomfortable, Hagelund's Deformity is usually easily treated. Sporting goods stores that sell and repair skates have hydraulic tools that can punch out the specific area of the boot that is causing the friction. A simple felt donut pad can also be used to protect the area from further irritation and prevent future occurrences of this common skating injury.

Playing at Madison Square Garden in New York was always a treat. The games were often held on a Saturday night and often only three or four hours after a concert or circus performance had taken place. It was not unusual to walk by occupied tiger and lion cages on the way to the ice surface before the game. On bad nights, we noticed areas where the ice was completely chipped away down to the concrete. That was just during warmup! The icemakers had the horrendous job of making quality ice in such an impossibly short amount of time. To this day I am still amazed that there are not more serious injuries in New York simply because of the poor ice quality!

PROTECTION

From a risk management standpoint, it is becoming increasingly important for coaches to inspect ice quality before allowing their teams to set foot in the rink. Large cracks, uneven ridges, and chipped-out areas increase the chances of players sustaining ankle or foot injuries.

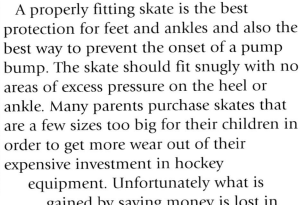

Many secondhand skates can provide just as much support for a young player as do new skates that cost three times as much!

A properly fitting skate is the best protection for feet and ankles and also the best way to prevent the onset of a pump bump. The skate should fit snugly with no areas of excess pressure on the heel or ankle. Many parents purchase skates that are a few sizes too big for their children in order to get more wear out of their expensive investment in hockey equipment. Unfortunately what is gained by saving money is lost in protection and skill development. Not only does this practice increase the risk for injury, but also the children have even more difficulty improving their skating! A great way to save money on hockey equipment is to purchase secondhand skates each year. Many secondhand skates can provide just as much support for a young player as do new skates that cost three times as much! The cost is minimal, especially when factoring in the trade-in value, and the child can improve skills using properly fitting skates at all times.

A Final Word about Injuries

Mothers of injured hockey players often complain to me about the physical nature of the game, hoping that their sons or daughters will quit for the sake of safety. I always recommend that a child continue to play if he or she is still interested, as hockey can be a highly exciting and enjoyable lifelong sport. However, a few points should be kept in mind to ensure the optimum in safety:

- All teams should have and practice an **Emergency Action Plan**.
- Never move a player with a possible head or neck injury.
- Use the RICE principle for soft tissue injuries.
- If an injury has not healed in three to four days, then see a physician for evaluation.
- Full rehabilitation of an injury is vital for long-term hockey performance.

Chapter 7

8 - Fitness Training— On-ice and Dryland

For many years hockey coaches have focused primarily on the development of a player's technical skills. Countless on-ice drills have been developed to improve a player's skating ability, stickhandling, passing, shooting, and checking skills. Once players have developed satisfactory individual skills and have passed the age of about 10, coaches can then progress to team-oriented drills that include offensive breakouts, defensive zone positioning, power plays, and penalty killing strategies. This is the sequence of skill development that most coaches can offer players, since they see them for only one or two practice hours per week during the season. Unfortunately, many coaches overlook an essential component to the success of a young player's hockey experience simply because of the nature of practice scheduling during a season. That essential missing component is fitness training.

With the increasing academic and professional opportunities for young hockey players, there has also been an increased emphasis on more ice time for players, allowing for even more development of individual and team hockey skills. Unfortunately, in most cases, more ice time also leads to a higher cost of playing the game and that is already a major barrier to participation for many families. Consequently, it is essential that creative coaches look at inexpensive options to develop their players' skills from the standpoint of physical conditioning in order to augment their on-ice hockey skills.

Like well-organized hockey practices, dryland-training sessions can be fun for both players and coaches. Hockey players who develop a positive attitude toward fitness and conditioning early in their training build a solid foundation for their future level of fitness, whether they choose to progress to elite levels of hockey or not.

FIVE COMPONENTS OF FITNESS TRAINING

There are five main components of physical fitness training that contribute to optimal hockey performance:

1. **Speed**
2. **Flexibility**
3. **Strength**
4. **Power**
5. **Endurance**

In this section, each of these components is explained in detail relative to its importance to physical fitness. Strategies for promoting these components and on-ice and off-ice drill favorites are provided as well. More drills and strategies will be provided in *Drill Solutions* and other books in the *LifeSport* series. See the Appendix for a sample dryland-training schedule that can be used as a template for these important training sessions.

Speed

The game of hockey is a dynamic, fast-paced competition that demands exceptional skating speed. If all other skills are equal when comparing two players, then the athlete with better speed can pick up loose pucks more quickly, avoid body checks more easily, and respond to game situations more effectively.

There are only two fundamental ways to increase skating speed:

1. *Increase the number of strides a player takes over a certain period of time.*
2. *Increase the stride length.*

In the first instance, players who develop stronger muscles as they grow are naturally able to extend their skating legs faster and then recover to a mid-stance position more quickly. Every player who grows from age five to fifteen becomes a faster skater simply because of an increased physical presence; however, coaches have many creative options both on and off the ice to instruct players on how to increase leg speed.

Players can develop longer strides by

1. *learning proper technique and*
2. *developing stronger thigh muscles.*

Often young players do not learn the proper technique of full leg extension while pushing out

THE TECHNICAL, THE PHYSICAL, AND THE MENTAL GAME

I met my wife, Kathy Vogt, at the 1980 Winter Olympics in Lake Placid, New York. These were her second Olympic Games representing Canada as a speed skater. I tell my friends that I was instantly attracted to her because she was the only girl I knew who could skate faster than I could. (I suppose there were thousands but she was the only one I was interested in!) A few years later Kathy came to visit me in Edmonton and after watching the Oilers play a few games she was quick to point out that really only one player on the Oilers had an almost-perfect skating technique. She did not know his name but he wore number seven and played defense. She meant Paul Coffey, who is remembered as one of the smoothest and speediest skaters ever to play the game. In speed skating where hundredths of a second are often the difference between a gold medal and the middle of the pack, Kathy had been trained for eight years with the National Team to keep her knees bent as close to 90° as possible. This position allows for maximal thrust from each stride, thus speed skaters can achieve the fastest speed possible. I always keep that experience firmly in my mind when I am coaching young hockey players so that I remember to use drills that challenge them to keep their knees bent low with legs extended fully through their strides.

Kathy Vogt, 1977 World Championships

away from the body during a skating stride. Repetitive practice on the ice using dynamic drills give players a better understanding of the importance of a full and correct skating stride. While performing skating drills it is important to stress that keeping knees bent while skating allows for longer and more effective strides. It does, however, take stronger thigh muscles to maintain a bent-knee position while skating, so for younger skaters, their relative muscle weakness is a barrier to faster skating. An off-ice program for players of all ages helps to reduce this barrier and if it is done correctly there should be minimal potential for overuse injury.

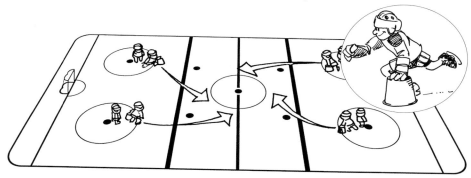

ON-ICE DRILL FAVORITE FOR SPEED

Four Corner Circle Pail Relay

Although there are many excellent drills for improving skating speed, my favorite is borrowed from the world of speed skating. The "Four-Corner Circle Pail Relay" is an exciting and fun drill for players of all ages.

Objectives

- to work on increasing speed
- to develop better control on both inside and outside skate edges

Key Teaching Points

- Encourage bent knee positioning with quick crossovers.

Description

Divide players into four groups, one group for each of the circles in the end zones. The players in each group line up directly behind each other with the first one at the top of the circle looking towards the center of the ice. Each group has a pail that is placed upside down on the ice. On the whistle, the first player in each group places an inside hand on the pail and skates as quickly as possible towards the center circle. The four players skate around the center circle in the same direction, each ensuring that the inside hand is holding the pail and the arm is extended to the inside of the circle rather than out in front. Having traveled a full circle each skates back to the respective "home" circle and delivers the pail to the next player in line. The drill is complete when all players have skated once around the center circle. The head coach stands in the middle of the center circle to ensure all players skate in the proper direction and that they stay on the outside of the circle.

With this drill players develop a heightened sense of skating in a bent knee position and they feel more comfortable with quicker foot movements when crossing over. Both are important components of increasing overall skating speed.

Drill Option

One player pushes the pail while a teammate sits on top of it. The extra resistance provides excellent practice for power training for the pusher while the player sitting on the pail must maneuver his feet to stay in line while maintaining proper balance as he glides around the circle. Players have lots of fun with this drill especially when coaches are flexible and do

not take the competition seriously. While they may lose their balance or run into other teams while moving around the circle, players gain confidence coping with new challenges.

"A" "B" "C"

OFF-ICE DRILL FAVORITE FOR SPEED

ABCs of Running

Although the technique of running is vastly different from skating technique, the same principles of foot speed and stride length apply. Sprinters and middle distance runners regularly work on their running technique by separating the running stride into its components. This is called the ABCs of running:

- **A** is the motion where a runner quickly brings a knee up in front of the hips. Once that knee extends to a position straight out from the body, then

- **B** is the accelerated motion that brings the foot down to the ground. That same foot then becomes the weight-bearing foot and it supports the body's weight during forward motion. Finally, when that foot eventually leaves the ground to begin another step,

- **C** is the action of the knee quickly bending up, almost attempting to kick oneself in the buttocks.

These three components of the running stride are important because when a runner practices them individually and repetitively while progressing slowly to an integrated set of high-speed movements, amazing speed gains can be achieved. Many experts believe that the running speed progression is also beneficial for sports like skating where foot speed and stride length are the determining factors in increasing the speed of movement.

Objective

• to work on increasing skating speed

Key Teaching Points

• Encourage proper technique.
• Encourage explosive movement.

Description

Teach the ABCs of running in a park or in a gym. Arrange the players in a line side by side. On a signal, all participants work on one of the running components for a distance of 20 to 30 meters. It is important to progress slowly because the ABC maneuvers can be difficult for players who are unaccustomed to them. With regular practice, however, most players will become more comfortable with the ABC movements of running.

To make the drill more fun, organize relay races using only one of the movements. Emphasize explosive leg movement and technique rather than winning or losing!

''A'' of Running

Remember that skating speed increases with quicker leg movement and longer strides. Both skills are refined with this drill.

Drill Option

Try a combination of movements over a similar course (once players are comfortable with all three individual movements). These drills not only help the hockey players in their on-ice pursuits but also are valuable for other sports such as baseball, basketball, and football.

Flexibility

Flexibility is defined as the range of motion around a particular joint in the body. There are two main types of flexibility exercises:

1. *static*
2. *dynamic*

Stretching exercises can be further subdivided into active stretching, where the athlete's muscles are working during the stretch, and passive stretching, where an external force is applied to the body to enhance the stretch. During a static stretch the body or parts of the body are not actively moving. Examples of this type of stretch are shown in Chapter 5 "Stretching, Warmup, and Cooldown" and are appropriate flexibility exercises for early in a training program. During a dynamic stretch the body is actively moving, particularly in a manner that imitates the motions specific to the athlete's sport. It is the dynamic type of flexibility exercise that will be described in this section. Dynamic, active flexibility drills can be effectively used to help reduce injuries and improve performance.

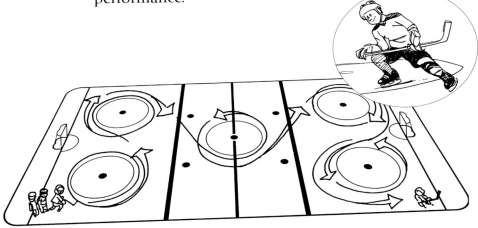

ON-ICE DRILL FAVORITE FOR FLEXIBILITY

Five Circle Skating with Elbow on Knee

The goal of every coach is to produce faster, more agile, and more powerful skaters. One of the key factors in improving skating speed and power is the development of a more exaggerated bent leg posture during a skating stride. The "Five Circle Skating Drill" is a popular drill for use early in a practice so that players work on crossover turns, balance, and coordination. An interesting twist to this familiar drill entices the skaters to become more comfortable in a bent-knee position while at the same time challenging them to increase dynamic flexibility through the hip joints during the skating stride. This is not an easy drill for first-time participants, but if done regularly, then every player will soon feel more comfortable and as a result, skating speed, flexibility, and power will improve substantially.

Objective

- to increase dynamic flexibility through the hip joints during the skating stride

Key Teaching Points

- Keep one elbow on the inside knee.
- Extend push-off leg fully.

Description

Line up players in one corner of the rink. On a whistle the first three begin skating around the perimeter of the closest circle. Players attempt to keep the inside elbow placed directly on their inside knees. This position encourages skaters to remain in a more efficient skating position with legs bent as close to 90° as possible.

Encourage skaters to push off with their outside legs to maximum extension, using the longest stride possible. When the first three skaters have completed the first circle, they then skate to the adjacent end zone circle, progress to the center circle, and then finally on to the circles at the other end of the rink in a similar fashion.

The next three skaters should begin the drill once the previous group completes the first circle. It is important to stress that this drill is not intended to be a race, but rather an opportunity to work on skating technique while focusing on full leg extension in their skating stride.

Drill Option

Have each player handle a puck with the outside arm while skating around the circles. This progression helps players gain a more complete understanding of efficient skating form and it also increases their ability to control a puck while maintaining proper skating form. It is also an excellent opportunity for players to practice changing hands during one-arm stickhandling because, although the need to control the stick with the nondominant hand does not happen often, players will have the opportunity to practice it before circumstances demand it in a game situation.

OFF-ICE DRILL FAVORITE FOR FLEXIBILITY

Half Moon Drill

There are many dryland drills that enhance skating speed and flexibility and the "Half Moon Drill" is a

favorite because it produces an increased dynamic flexibility in almost all ranges of leg movement. It can be performed in a gym or at home and it can be an important addition to the development of a committed hockey player's dryland program.

Objective

• to enhance skating speed and flexibility

Key Teaching Points

• Keep the weight-bearing knee bent.
• Extend the leg completely.

Description

Have a group of players spread out in a gym or other large room. On a whistle, all bend one knee and put all their weight on the bent leg as they extend the other leg as far forward and straight as possible. Once fully extended forward, the player then moves the straight leg in a semicircle fashion until the leg is fully extended behind the player. During this circular movement, the player attempts to stretch the leg as far away from the body as possible in order to simulate maximal stride length. The player should point the toe as far as possible during the half moon movement to simulate a full skating push off. Repeat the movement several times before switching to the other leg.

Drill Options

The difficult aspect of this drill is that younger players are often unable to keep the weight-bearing leg bent at a reasonable angle for any length of time.

1. Beginning skaters or skaters who wish to practice maximal leg extension may lean down and grasp a box or chair that is at or around knee height. The aid allows players to practice the maneuver in a lower bent-knee position and also allows them to practice greater leg extensions as they perform the semicircle movement.

2. More experienced skaters can use even lower supports in order to place additional stress on the leg muscles during this dynamic stretch. As players progress through the drill, one-legged balance will improve and a box or chair will no longer be needed.

Strength

On analyzing the game of hockey, it is easy to see the importance of strength—the ability to exert force against resistance. Whether battling for a puck in the corner or achieving good screening position in front of the opposition's net, strength is a necessity for

When I was a child, my favorite NHL star was Bobby Hull of the Chicago Black Hawks. With his flowing blond hair and amazingly hard slap shot, he was always a treat to watch on television. When he was asked how he developed such a hard shot, Bobby would explain, "from throwing bales of hay back on the farm." We would laugh at such a ridiculous notion! Here was a great star getting stronger with farm work. Many years later when I considered the type of repetitive stresses on his shoulders, forearms, and back from this type of work, I realized that Bobby's unusual form of summer training was probably more sport specific than that of many athletes who spend time working out in a gym.

ultimate performance. In the past when strength training was mentioned in the context of hockey, weightlifting with bench presses and biceps curls was usually the order of the day. Although weightlifting exercises can certainly promote strength gains in older athletes, it is not recommended that growing players use weights for strength training. As a result, more innovative and effective strength exercises have been developed that can be used by hockey players of all ages.

The purpose of strength training for younger athletes is not to develop larger and bulkier muscles. In fact, if the purpose of strength training was to help players to bulk up, then these athletes would be at great risk of overuse injuries and potential long-term side effects. Significant stress on the open growth plates in the bones of young athletes can cause arrested growth as well as long term joint pain. Young players can, however, significantly improve their muscle strength without adding extra muscle tissue or exposing themselves to potentially damaging injuries.

ON-ICE DRILL FAVORITE FOR STRENGTH

Bull in the Ring

Developing an on-ice drill that works specifically to improve strength is not easy. Almost every drill incorporates some aspect of strength development, whether it includes shooting, battling for position in front of the net, or trying to win a one-on-one battle for the puck. "The Bull in the Ring Drill" isolates a strength challenge between individual players.

Objective

• to enhance strength

Key Teaching Points

• Defending player maintains a strong tripod stance.
• Pushing player attempts to push opponent off balance.

Description

Divide players into pairs according to their size and ability. Each coach takes half of the pairings and lines them up outside of one of the circles. To set up the drill, the first pair enters the circle with one

My former teammate, Mark Messier, is another great example of how off-season strength training need not be boring or tedious. Mark had one of the most well-defined, muscular bodies in the game and at every training camp he would arrive fresh and strong as an ox. When I asked how he kept himself in such good shape in the off-season, he would simply reply with a wry smile, "water-skiing." Thinking back, I can't imagine a better way to develop upper body, forearm, and leg strength for hockey than with the high powered forces gained when water-skiing at maximum intensity. With Mark, you knew that everything he did was "to the MAX!"

player assuming a tripod stance (i.e. stick held firmly on the ice). The other player holds onto the first player's hips. On the whistle, the first player tries to maintain a strong position as close to the circle dot as possible, while the other tries to push him out of the circle. After five to ten seconds, the coach blows a whistle to conclude the drill. The timing is purposely kept short to encourage 100% intensity from the players. Pairs continue to rotate into each circle, with all players trying both offensive and defensive positions.

Drill Options

Have the players use no sticks during the challenge. This option removes the benefit of the tripod stance and effectively reinforces its importance in a game situation.

OFF-ICE DRILL FAVORITE FOR STRENGTH

Wall Sits

Athletes in many sports have used "Wall Sits" when their athletic performance requires increased strength in the thigh muscles. In hockey, stronger thigh muscles translate into a lower knee bend and stronger leg push while striding. The beauty of this drill is that it can be done anywhere at anytime, as the only equipment necessary is a wall.

Objective

• to increase thigh muscle strength

Key Teaching Points

- Keep knees and hips bent at 90°.

Description

Players can do "Wall Sits"
individually or as a team.
Each player finds an open area
on a wall. On a signal, players
slide their buttocks down the
wall until knees and hips are
at a 90° angle and they hold
the position for as long as
possible. Players fold their
arms across the front of their
chests so that the arms cannot
be used for extra support.
They can keep a record of how
long they are able to maintain
the wall sit position. As leg

strength improves, the length of time a player can
remain in a bent leg position will increase.

Drill Option

An interesting option is the "Partner Wall Sit."
Select players of equal size and ability and have
them perform a wall sit while standing back to back.
It is still important that their knees and hips are bent
at 90°, their arms remain crossed and their backs
stay right together supporting their bent leg stance.
Making this drill a competition is a great way to
have fun and encourage the players to do their best.

Power

Sports commentators often describe how a
particular player has a powerful stride and the ability
to break through opposing defensemen with ease.
Power is a component of movement that is
produced through a combination of speed and

strength. Both are required to produce the explosive stride that is so important for elite level hockey players. In minor hockey levels it is not uncommon to see a young player who can skate fast, but is knocked off the puck easily. It is also common to see players who have considerable upper and lower body strength but who skate slowly, making them less effective. To ensure the most success in the game it is necessary to expose young athletes to regular on- and off-ice drills that emphasize power development. Having one or more power forwards on a team is a valuable advantage if the team is focused on dominating games with fundamental skills and skating prowess.

Power drills need not be tedious or boring. In fact, a well-prepared coach can use enjoyable, challenging drills to enhance power in a way that the players will look forward to them in the next dryland session.

ON-ICE DRILL FAVORITE FOR POWER

Push-Pull Skating Drill

Power is a combination of speed and strength; therefore, an effective power drill must naturally challenge players to develop increased strength while skating at full speed. The many variations of the "Push-Pull Skating Drill" do just that.

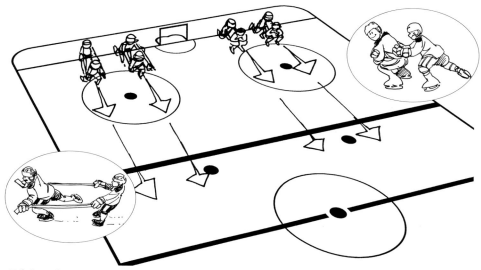

Objective

• to enhance power by building strength at full speed

Key Teaching Points

• Skate at full intensity.
• Allow sufficient rest between drill repetitions to ensure that the speed component of the drill is not compromised.

Description

Divide players into pairs relative to their size and ability. Line the pairs on the goal line at one end of the rink.

1. Push Drill

Using no sticks, the lead player faces forward, assuming a full bent-knee position. Coaches may request that the lead players keep their elbows directly on their knees to promote a proper bent-knee skating

position. The second—pushing player—places hands on the lead player's hips. On a whistle, pushing players skate as quickly as possible down the length of the rink, pushing the lead player forward. At the opposite end of the rink, the two players exchange positions and repeat the drill.

2. Pull Drill

With sticks, paired players line up one behind the other with both players facing forward at one end of

the rink. The lead player grasps one end of both sticks, one in each hand, while the rear player holds the other ends of the sticks. On the whistle, the lead player skates as fast as possible down the length of the rink, maintaining a bent-knee stance and full leg thrust when striding. The rear player is either pulled down the ice or may apply some resistance by partially braking with skates. At the opposite end of the rink, the players exchange positions and repeat the drill.

Drill Options

A reasonable progression to any power drill is one that either increases the speed of the drill or the resistance in the drill. Since these drills are already designed to be performed at full speed, increased resistance is the only option.

1. Hand-to-Shoulder Push Drill

Instead of beginning in a forward skating position, the lead player faces the pushing player. With arms straight and placed on the pushing player's shoulders, the lead player resists forward skating movement, making it harder to advance down the ice. The lead player can adjust the amount of pressure applied so that the pushing player maintains some momentum while skating down the ice but is still challenged to use powerful, bent-leg strides to advance.

2. Pull Drill Variations

To increase the skating resistance in this drill, several options are available. The rear player can increase skating resistance by

a) using a snowplow skating action to slow the skating progress,

b) kneeling down while being pulled, or

c) lying face down with arms extended while being pulled.

OFF-ICE DRILL FAVORITE FOR POWER

Lateral Skater's Stride

There are many dryland drills that can be used for power development. In sports such as track and field, bobsled, skiing, and basketball, athletes can develop powerful leg muscles with relatively simple yet effective drills like the "Lateral Skater's Stride."

Objective

- to improve skating power

Key Teaching Points

- Maintain proper form.
- Maintain good one-foot balance.

Description

The "Lateral Skater's Stride" can be performed on any flat, dry surface indoors or outdoors. Apply two lines of tape on the ground approximately one meter apart. Hockey sticks can also be used to mark out the boundaries.

Players begin by balancing on one foot outside of one line. They push off with that leg sideways, landing on the opposite leg outside of the opposite line. As the players land on one foot, encourage them to cushion the landing by bending the landing knee as low as they can while remaining balanced. They then bring the other foot into a neutral position directly under the body. Players repeat the movements as they work their way slowly down the lines. When they get to the end, they walk back to the start and prepare to repeat the drill. A combination of balance and powerful leg muscles is required to perform this drill effectively.

Drill Options

1. Begin with the lines less than one meter apart for young players and slowly increase the distance. The distance between the lines can be increased progressively in order to challenge more experienced skaters.

2. Have players try to touch the opposite elbow to the landing knee as it is bending and supporting full body weight. This elbow-to-knee contact ensures that the player's center of gravity is low and the knees are bent correctly.

Endurance

Endurance is defined as the ability to sustain or repeat intense effort. In a dynamic game like hockey, skating intensity and checking effort is the key to a player's success. In fact, endurance is the cornerstone for all other physical performance factors. Without endurance, the other physical components of speed, strength, power, and flexibility are all less effective. The nature of endurance-enhancing activities is that they must last for an extended period of time to work the body's cardiovascular and respiratory systems—the heart and lungs. The challenge, however, is to organize endurance activities that do not become boring or stale, otherwise that eventually leads to decreased practice intensity.

One of the side benefits of successfully exposing young players to endurance exercises is that longer duration, lower intensity activities provide protection from future risk of heart attacks and stroke. What a valuable legacy the game can give to young players when they can experience the benefits of regular exercise in a sport that can truly become a lifelong activity.

Note: Endurance drills of the type provided here should be done later in a practice. If done properly, then they tend to fatigue players; therefore, technical drills designed to improve passing, stickhandling, and shooting should be performed before endurance drills.

ON-ICE DRILL FAVORITE FOR ENDURANCE

Two-on-Two Inside Blue Line

It is important that endurance activities last for extended periods of time. The "Two-on-Two Inside Blue Line" drill simulates a real game situation where players must skate hard for 30 to 45 seconds and then rest on the bench. Because this drill divides the technical playing skills into their fundamental components, namely skating, stickhandling, passing, shooting, and checking, players make valuable gains in endurance while participating in a fun yet challenging competition.

Objective

- to increase endurance while participating in a fun and challenging competition

Key Teaching Points

- Move into open areas.
- Maintain proper one-on-one positioning.
- Make quick transitions between groups.

Description

Divide players into two groups, each located at opposite ends of the rink. Groups may be based on skill so that players compete against teammates with relatively similar skill levels. Further divide each group into two teams and line them up just outside the respective blue lines. Slide a puck into the offensive zone and following a whistle cue, the first two players of each group skate quickly to gain possession of the puck. The two pairs battle for the puck and try to score on the goalie. Both teams are on the offense, but if the goalie gains control of the puck, then he releases it quickly behind the net. After 20 to 30 seconds blow the whistle and as the pairs quickly skate out of the zone, the next two players in each line skate towards the loose puck to try to gain control. The drill is continuous and if a goal is scored, then the goalie simply releases the puck behind the net to resume play. Continue the drill for 10 to 15 minutes so that players can gain endurance benefits.

Drill Option

Use a three-on-three format. With only fourteen to sixteen skaters on most minor hockey teams, this progression means reduced rest periods between intense play, thus increasing the players' endurance benefits.

OFF-ICE DRILL FAVORITE FOR ENDURANCE

Ultimate Football

It cannot be overemphasized that, in order to encourage maximum effort and high interest from players, endurance exercises must be fun. "Ultimate Football" is a great example of a fun, high intensity drill, because players must play hard for extended

periods of time. They also tend to enjoy the challenge without fully realizing how much they are improving their endurance.

Objective

• to improve cardiovascular endurance through intense, enjoyable dryland competition

Key Teaching Points

• Focus on team play.
• Move into open areas.
• Work on strategy.

Description

"Ultimate Football" is similar to the increasingly popular Frisbee game called "Ultimate." Divide players into two teams on a field or in a gym. Mark the sideline boundaries and goal posts at each end using pylons. The object of the game is to throw a small soft football to teammates while slowly advancing up the field. A team scores a touchdown when they successfully complete a pass thrown from one side of the goal posts to the other. The ball must be caught by a teammate in midair. The defending team can intercept throws simply by knocking the ball out of the air to the ground. When a throw is knocked down or the ball is dropped, the defending team gains possession of the ball and begins its advance down the field in the opposite direction.

One important rule in "Ultimate Football" is that the player in possession of the ball cannot move at all, in any direction. This forces teammates to move into open areas of the field and encourages smart passing in order to advance the ball offensively. The parallels of "Ultimate Football" to hockey are strong and young hockey players soon begin to understand the importance of supporting the ball carrier and the effectiveness of short, quick passes in order to advance their offensive position.

Drill Option

Allow players three steps after catching the ball before throwing the football to a teammate. This progression allows for a higher tempo and an increased endurance benefit.

Note: In both variations there is little need for a referee since the rules are straightforward. Either the player catches the ball and retains possession or the ball is dropped or knocked to the ground in which case the opposing team gains ball possession.

A Final Word about Fitness Training

In the next ten years, dryland training for improved hockey performance will most certainly come into its own. Due to the rising cost of ice time for hockey teams, innovative coaches will look to local gyms or

available parks to establish a fitness-training program for their players. This will allow the important on-ice sessions to focus primarily on skill and team development. The combination of physical and technical enhancement is important for complete hockey player development.

Refer to the Appendix for a sample dryland-training practice plan that can be used as a template for coaches who are interested in adding a dryland-training component to their practice schedules.

The Mental Game

attitudes,
mental preparation

THE MENTAL GAME

The final and possibly most important section delves into the attitudes, philosophies, life skills, and mental toughness that have always been a part of the game but have often been overlooked in many sporting venues. Hockey is not only a game played on an ice rink, it is also a game played in the minds and hearts of the players involved.

It is a well-known fact that young people become involved in sports of their choice primarily because they want to have fun with their friends. This is certainly true of hockey. However, a great coach understands this purpose and can build on it by teaching not only skills, but also providing a fun, positive learning environment where children build self-esteem, self-confidence, discipline, and the long-lost art of sportsmanship.

The game has changed greatly over the years. There are concerns about rampant violence and abuse in what was always considered to be a pure sport. Coaches and parents must be sensitive to these issues and try to provide players with an experience that not only teaches them to play a great game, but also helps them gain life skills that will make them both great players and great people! Our role as parents, coaches, and administrators must be one in which we value the involvement of every young person in our sport. All of our decisions in and around the hockey rink must be focused on how we can keep every athlete playing and enjoying the sport for many years to come.

9 - Attitudes in Hockey

The game of hockey has changed greatly over the past twenty years. Gone are the days of recreational skill development on an outdoor pond or rink with no coaches, fans, or scoreboards involved. Hockey has become much more sophisticated, with multimillion dollar contracts up for grabs and with them, the inevitable pressures and ultimate disappointments.

Most people who reflect on the game and its importance in Canadian and North American society realize that the goal of amateur hockey should not be simply a route for sculpting players into NHL prototypes. The sheer number of participants in this great game demands the setting of loftier goals for our maturing players. Developing self-confidence and self-esteem, challenging one's discipline and determination, developing a healthy respect for opposition and officials, learning how to both win

In 1980 I had the privilege to share the company of Father David Bauer, a former Basilian priest and head of Canada's National Hockey Team in the 1960s. He believed that participating in hockey developed valuable life skills in young men and women—the ability to compete to the best of their ability, to try as hard as they can to win, but more importantly to develop into great human beings who will become tomorrow's leaders. His favorite saying that I will never forget and that I often repeat to the young players I coach in hockey, baseball, and other sports was, "Make use of technique, but let the spirit prevail." It is a simple statement, but one that is often ignored in many factions of amateur hockey. We are consumed with the need to teach young players the skills, but we often forget to reveal to them the real beauty of all sport participation—the burning desire, the enthusiasm, and the spirit that separates the good athletes from the truly great ones! As hockey continues to take the spotlight on the world stage, coaches should look for opportunities not just to develop great players, but rather to develop intuitive thinkers, dominant leaders, and truly great people!

and lose like a champion, and most importantly, having fun—these are qualities that every hockey player must have the chance to experience and develop individually.

Why then, are so many hockey coaches preoccupied with solely teaching players how to win the game? Often overlooked is the fact that learning the intricacies of the game is an effective way to use a child's hockey experience to mold them into a responsible, caring, dedicated, disciplined, trusting, and happy individual. Should this not be the ultimate goal in hockey? It is a goal attainable by all players, not just the best.

Some hard-liners say that kids must be toughened up—skate them until they drop and punish them with endless skating practices for losing a game. Others wonder whether this attitude enhances a player's hockey experience or destroys it. If parents, coaches, managers, and fans have clear goals for children in hockey, then with just a little self-reflection, the choice about what children should ultimately learn from the game is apparent.

This chapter is about focusing on the positive; it is about building attitudes in young men and women that will carry them throughout the rest of their lives. These are the less tangible skills that players come away with. This chapter provides suggestions that any coach can use to give every young athlete they encounter a positive hockey experience. Some of the ideas and concepts presented here may overlap. Many of these ideas and suggestions do bear repeating since they are so important for giving the children in your charge your best effort while asking them for their best.

"Make use of technique, but let the spirit prevail."
–Father David Bauer

Coaching Philosophy

Twenty years from now, few former Peewee hockey players will remember whether they came in first or second place in a spring hockey tournament. On the other hand, the memory of the sting at being verbally abused by a coach for making a bad play that cost the game endures, sometimes for a player's whole life.

Human memory is amazing, primarily because we remember significant events in our lives and we tend to forget the seemingly unimportant ones. I can certainly attest to that. Only a few years after winning five Stanley Cup championships, I have a hard time remembering which team we beat to win each Stanley Cup. Don't even ask who we beat in the Campbell Conference Finals all those years! However, I will never forget the time when I was thirteen and my hockey coach, Wayne Gamble, asked me to go out and start his car after practice on a cold wintry day. What a thrill it was that one of my

THE TECHNICAL, THE PHYSICAL, AND THE MENTAL GAME

greatest role models showed enough confidence in me to toss me his car keys. Unfortunately, at thirteen, the only thing I knew about cars was how to turn the key. Little did I know that Wayne owned a vehicle with a standard transmission! Luckily my father was watching my attempts to start the car while it was in gear and came to my rescue.

Coaches have the power and the responsibility to instill character, confidence, respect, and the ability to lead in every player during every season. In North America, if twenty hockey coaches were asked the secrets of their success, there would likely be twenty different answers. One of the beauties of life is the amazing variety of attitudes and approaches that can be taken to any task.

When it comes to coaching, however, there are ways that all coaches can provide the ultimate coaching experience for their players. These are:

- **Plan fun activities for games and practices.**

- **Create a positive learning environment.**

- **Be consistent; treat all players fairly.**

- **Be well prepared for practices and games.**

- **Be a positive role model for your players.**

- **Work together with the opposing coach and the game officials to provide the most enjoyable experience for all the players.**

- **Include players in the decision making process during the season.**

- **Teach success as an attitude—players can learn as much from a loss as they can from a win.**

PLAN FUN ACTIVITIES FOR GAMES AND PRACTICES

In order to keep young people playing hockey, coaches must ensure that they enjoy their experience. To do that, games that teach the skills of skating, balance, speed, conditioning, and so on can be included in each practice. Teaching hockey skills as well as the intricacies of the game can be a great way to show children the camaraderie and spirit that develops in sporting teams. An environment of fun along with competition can only enhance their experience. Remember that the number one reason why kids play hockey is because they want to have fun with their friends!

Included in this book are instructions for many fun games and skill drills that can be incorporated into practices. These can mostly be found in the Chapter 2, "Individual Skills" and Chapter 8, "Fitness Training."

CREATE A POSITIVE LEARNING ENVIRONMENT

Even the best NHL players make mistakes both on and off the ice. So do young players just learning the game. Coaches must expect errors to be made during a game; however, responding in a positive way can turn mistakes into learning opportunities. Starting out with a positive remark before making constructive suggestions about ways that players can improve is a good way to take some of the sting out of what may be viewed as criticism. A good rule of thumb is to try to give three positive remarks for  every constructive suggestion or remark about an error! Players should never be afraid to make mistakes, because that is the only way they will learn and get better. Therefore, how the coach approaches a player will determine just what that player actually learns from a mistake. Will the player learn to play it safe in order to avoid making mistakes in the future or learn from the coach's suggestions and in a similar situation risk trying something new in order to improve his play? Coaches have a great deal of power over the way players handle their mistakes, both positively and negatively.

BE CONSISTENT; TREAT ALL PLAYERS FAIRLY

The best rewards a player can get from hockey are the feelings of excitement and companionship that come with being part of a team. As a result there is nothing more devastating to a team than when some players are treated differently. It is natural that a coach might feel differently about certain players. There are players on every team who seem to know what the coach wants almost before it is mentioned and who learn concepts quickly and easily. There are also those who cannot seem to understand certain concepts or drills no matter how hard they try. Even though not all players are goal scorers or stars, each one is an important part of the team.

All players, even the favorites, sense when a coach treats their teammates differently and that sends a wrong message to the entire group—that some players are more important to the team than others. While it can be difficult to treat all players the same way, even a player who does not have the skill to be on the power play may, with practice and patient instruction, become a valuable penalty killer for the team.

The best amateur hockey coaches believe that each player is as valuable as the next, and should be treated as such! It is up to the coach to see that all players develop to their potential and the only way that can happen is in a positive learning environment where all players are equally valued.

BE PREPARED FOR PRACTICES AND GAMES

On a practice or a game day, coaches expect players to have their equipment on, their skates done up, and be ready to hit the ice as soon as the Zamboni is clear. The players, meanwhile, should be able to expect that the coach is well prepared to run an effective, organized, and efficient practice where they will have fun with their teammates and improve their skills. Planning for each practice as well as long-term planning for the complete season practice schedule ensures the best learning experience for all the players. A well-organized practice makes efficient use of time, keeps all the players moving, and ensures that nobody gets bored during the session.

Many coaches have a general plan that they follow for each practice. They use specific drills to teach players the sequence of individual skills necessary to play the game, adding more difficult progressions as the players master the simpler drills and introducing more complex drills that closely simulate game situations. Many creative drills and progressions are included in Chapter 2, "Individual Skills." The Appendix contains sample practice plans and a blank template that can be photocopied or adapted to a coach's personal style. The section called "Practice Organization" in the latter part of this chapter provides practical suggestions on planning practices and getting the most out of the ice time available.

BE A POSITIVE ROLE MODEL

Coaching hockey is a great opportunity to teach players the skills of the game. However, it is just as important to teach them about discipline, commitment, respect for the opposition and referees, fair play, and of course, how much fun the game can be. Coaches who are consistent and fair in their dealings with players, the opposition, and the referees during the game quickly gain the respect of

all the players. By the same token, coaches who lose their tempers over bad calls, shout at referees, or get angry after bad plays are also modeling those behaviors for players, who then assume that these behaviors are acceptable. As a result, it is no surprise when this coach's player takes a retaliation penalty or is ejected from a game for swearing. All coaches are role models for their players, and a coach's behavior influences players' behavior, after all. The choice between being a great role model or the opposite is obvious!

In response to a questionable penalty call, inexperienced coaches may yell at the referee, laying blame for disrupting the flow of their team's play. More experienced coaches who are in control of their emotions and aware of the effect their response will have on their players may say nothing. Instead, they will talk to their players about bearing down even harder to kill the penalty. With these actions, the first coach is indirectly showing players that questioning authority is acceptable and promoted on his team. The latter coach, however, is using a challenging situation during a game to teach players that they can conquer adversity with discipline, hard work, and commitment, rather than by complaining.

I often ask players who complain about a perceived injustice on the ice if they have ever seen referees change their minds on calls simply because a team complains. Can you imagine the scenario, a referee saying, "I'm sorry. Now that I've heard your complaints, I've changed my mind about that tripping call"? Impossible! Complaining about a referee's call is about as worthwhile as selling ice to the Inuit.

YA KNOW WHAT.. YOU'RE RIGHT! I'VE CHANGED MY MIND.

WORK TOGETHER WITH THE OPPOSING COACH AND THE OFFICIALS

Even though the object of the game is to try to win, a strong coach can show team players that hockey is fun regardless of a win or a loss. A positive, upbeat attitude by all the adults involved means that both winners and losers can come away with a positive experience. Hockey experts do not judge a team's integrity and poise on how they win, but rather on how they handle losing, because invariably the best losers won't be for long!

Several simple strategies can show players that the opposing team and the referees are not their enemies, but rather an integral part of the game of hockey. Many teams will

have their captains shake hands with the opposition coaches before the game. If coaches rotate their captains, then this gives all the players a chance to extend a gesture of fair play and respect to the opposition. Having all players shake hands with the referees at the end of the game is also worthwhile. By encouraging players to extend a hand to the officials after the final buzzer, coaches are promoting the concept of fair play and also providing closure for that particular sporting endeavor. Any hard feelings can be forgotten and players are more apt to remember the great plays and excitement of the game rather than any perceived bad penalty calls.

Meeting with the referees and the opposing coaches before the game often reinforces that all are in a similar situation in the game, just trying to make the game as enjoyable as possible for the players. Personal contact allows both calm and aggressive coaches to keep involvement with their hockey team in perspective. Winning at all costs is good for no one, but rather a high intensity, close-scoring game that challenges all players on both teams should be the ultimate goal. After all, neither the losing team nor the winning team benefits from an 11 to 1 hockey game!

INCLUDE PLAYERS IN DECISION MAKING

Coaching is an important job. The coach is the overall leader who makes the decisions for the team about who plays where and when, about the proper strategy for each game, and about organizing good practices so that players get maximum benefit from their ice time. However, when it comes to minor decisions that do not affect the overall team plan, a strong coach tries to allow the players to become involved in the decision making process. Cleaning up the dressing room, deciding what time players need to be at the rink before a game, and whether to enter a tournament are decisions that can be made as a team. When players become involved in making decisions, then they become more accountable and more committed to the team.

THE TECHNICAL, THE PHYSICAL, AND THE MENTAL GAME

TEACH SUCCESS AS AN ATTITUDE

Hockey is a game where 50% of the players in any given game will go home as losers on the scoreboard. It is an undeniable fact, yet it is possible to turn a loss on the scoreboard into a positive learning experience. After a game many coaches use the time in the dressing room as an opportunity to teach the players how to improve their play for the next game, rather than tell them how poorly they played. All teachers (including coaches) watch for the teachable moments, that is, the moments when a learner is most receptive or when the motivation to learn comes from within. The postgame talk can be this optimum time when coaches can boost sagging morale by pointing out all the successful plays during the game in order to reinforce skill improvement. Drawing attention to ways that players or lines can improve their performance is important while the game is still fresh in their minds.

> *Hockey is a game where 50% of the players in any given game will go home as losers on the scoreboard...*

Rather than focusing on the disappointment of an overtime loss, experienced coaches can discuss the strong pressure the team had on the opposition before the goal was scored. They can point out how better execution may have resulted in a goal by their team and at the same time prepare players for a more consistent effort next game.

Following a 5 to 2 loss, experienced coaches will use their postgame talks to point out situations when the opposition scored and analyze how each player could react more effectively next time in a similar situation. They could talk about particular strategies on how to counteract the other team's strengths in the offensive zone in preparation for the next game. Finally, experienced coaches will comment positively on how well executed their goals were and single out players for their hard work throughout the game. Using this strategy, the players will be disappointed with the loss but will leave the dressing room on an otherwise positive note! The cup can truly be half full rather than half empty; it all depends on the coach's attitude.

The Making of Great Players and People

"It's amazing what can be accomplished when nobody cares who gets the credit."
–Clare Drake, University of Alberta Golden Bears Hockey Coach

If the only goal in the sport of hockey were to win every game, then coaching young athletes would be straightforward. Coaches would try to acquire the strongest players, would hold practices every day, and would try to schedule games against weaker teams in order to ensure success. This is certainly the goal of professional hockey organizations. However, most minor hockey coaches know that coaching a sport is also a valuable way to teach children important life skills.

Unfortunately, some players, parents, and coaches see what occurs in the National Hockey League and believe that a similar attitude should filter down to minor hockey. Although the game is the same, other parallels between the National Hockey League and minor hockey should be avoided. The National Hockey League represents the pinnacle of hockey talent and excitement. There is only one goal during the games—to win. NHL players never enter a game saying, "Let's get out there and have a good game." On the contrary, because NHL teams are so evenly matched and are comprised of the best players in the world, each team believes that success naturally comes in only one way, with a victory. Many people also consider the National Hockey League to be a business rather than a sporting organization, with a dollars-and-cents bottom line rather than a focus on the guiding principles of the game. Experiments with pucks that glow like comets for the benefit of television coverage or the rumor of a change to four fifteen-minute periods to accommodate the media are just two examples of the compromises being made to Corporate America!

Compare the previously mentioned elite levels of hockey to minor hockey, where there is a wide range of skill levels and abilities, both between teams and within each team. Certainly one of the goals of any game is to try to win, and it is exciting to see young players trying their utmost to emerge as the victors in a weekend contest. However, for these young boys and girls it is just as important that, along with the game, they learn important life skills. If coaches remember why most children play hockey—to have fun with their friends—then winning naturally takes a lower profile.

After playing hockey for thirty years, I continue to confirm that in every hockey game across the country, barring ties, half the players win and the other half loses. Imagine the wasted time if those on the losing team got absolutely nothing out of the game!

Consider some of the life skills that all players can learn, whether they are on the winning or losing team. Some of these are:

- **Self-Esteem**
- **Self-Confidence**
- **Discipline**
- **Learning How to Win or Lose**
- **Respect for the Opposition and Referees**
- **Having Fun**

SELF-ESTEEM

On examining society's problems with adolescents today, the list might include smoking, drug use, suicide, teenage pregnancy, and poor scholastic performance. In each of these significant problems, a lack of self-esteem is implicated. The ability to think positively about oneself and one's future potential is a powerful force that can be used to keep young people moving forward in their lives. In hockey, where positive experiences and reinforcement from coaches can enhance a feeling of self-worth, it is possible to prevent these problems by taking steps to enhance self-esteem.

How can a coach help develop a heightened self-esteem in all players?

1. *Focus on the positive aspects of a game—fun, not the negative aspects—losing.*
2. *Be less concerned about wins and more interested in improving skills.*
3. *Always try to make three positive remarks to a player for every negative comment or constructive suggestion.*

Self-esteem cannot be bought; it is an inherent, inborn characteristic. It is affected negatively or positively by every experience we have in life, including hockey. Learning the game of hockey in a positive environment can be a valuable tool for enhancing self-esteem.

When I coach a hockey team, one strategy for improving self-esteem that I use is rotating the captaincy. Rather than assign the "C" and "As" to specific players, I select captains based on prior attitude, performance, and effort. Knowing that in minor hockey, captains have virtually no role on the ice, I am not putting my team at a disadvantage by doing this. On the contrary, I give myself the opportunities to reward players for doing things that I believe are most valuable. I rarely award the captaincy to a player who scores three goals because I want to show my players that team play is much more important than individual scoring pursuits. There are many instances when a weaker player can be singled out as deserving of the captaincy, even if that player is not a dominant goal scorer. A timely blocked shot, an energetic back checking effort or an unselfish pass can often be the reason for making a certain player the captain for the next game. I keep track of which players have been captains and can easily make sure that each player gets equal opportunity to be a team leader. The ultimate reward for this strategy is watching a young person burst with pride at being singled out as a team leader. I know of no more effective way to boost a hockey player's self-esteem than with this simple tactic.

SELF-CONFIDENCE

Those who believe they can and those who believe they can't are both right!
–Anonymous

You may have observed a player just before a penalty shot who seems to be thinking, "I'm not very good at these" and then you watch the shot miss the net. It may be a cliché but it is often said, "Those who believe they can and those who believe they can't are both right!" The ability to make young athletes believe that they are truly good hockey players, whether they are or not, is a skill that great coaches develop over the years.

Minor hockey is not just designed for the great players. It is imperative that all interested players have the opportunity to enjoy this exciting game and to develop self-confidence at any skill level. Some coaches complain that it is difficult to build up the confidence of a player who has poor hockey skills and seems to hurt the team on almost every shift. However, coaches who care about each member of the team remember that these young children are indeed just children. These coaches believe that the glory of winning is of lesser importance than the glory of seeing young people blossom in a sport that they are just learning!

How is it possible to build the self-confidence of a young, rather unskilled hockey player who hardly touches the puck during a game? Intuitive and observant coaches can always pick out certain decisions, plays, or positions that a player has chosen that, although not producing a goal scoring opportunity, can be identified as the proper play in that situation. A winger staying on the inside of the opposing defenseman in the defensive zone, a center anticipating a pass in the offensive end, a defenseman following a scoring opportunity to the high slot looking for a rebound; all of these are decisions that can be rewarded with praise from one of the coaching staff.

Another effective way to improve the self-confidence of team players is to include a series of individual comments during the postgame talk. Making a positive comment about *each* player that focuses on some aspect of the game in which they performed well is important so that all leave feeling that they are contributing members of the team. If a coach does not have a positive comment about every player, then it is better to say nothing. What can a person say to a backup goalie who didn't even play in the game? "Great job! You didn't let one shot go by you!"

DISCIPLINE

Teachers would love the opportunity to teach a subject that students enjoy more than anything. All children become excited when they are able to choose what they want to learn. Coaches have a window of opportunity with hockey because those who are playing the game have chosen to be there. Thus, coaches have the

> *"If people knew how hard I worked to gain my mastery, they would not think it so wonderful at all."*
> *–Michelangelo*

chance to develop strong work habits, focused attention, and self-discipline in their players. Like teachers, hockey coaches are valuable role models and must continually show athletes by example how important these habits and life skills truly are. Imagine the confusion brought on by coaches who demand punctuality before games and practices, but who are consistently late themselves. Or consider coaches who command the players to respect the referee's decisions, but who regularly shout and complain at what they think are bad calls. Discipline is a valuable skill that, once acquired, will be useful throughout life. Experiences in hockey can either enhance a player's disciplined attitude or destroy it!

It is a daunting task for coaches but they must realize that every single thing they do in the dressing room or on the bench will be scrutinized by fifteen sets of eyes and ears. Every comment, every action, every bit of body language will be taken in by the players and processed and adapted to fit their view of life. Make sure that players see a consistent approach to the team goals and philosophies set out early in the season not just from the head coach but from the entire coaching staff. If you ask your players to be enthusiastic, be enthusiastic yourself; if you ask for discipline, be disciplined yourself; if you want them to have fun, have fun yourself!

LEARNING HOW TO WIN AND LOSE

From a coaching perspective, there's no question that it is easier to coach a winning team than a losing team. There are fewer complaints from the parents, the players are generally happier and one's profile as an accomplished coach is enhanced. Many experts believe, however, that a player can learn more from a loss than a win. From the physical standpoint, playing against stronger teams pushes individuals to play to their highest potential, a situation that ultimately makes better players. As well, playing against teams that are highly overmatched provides little challenge and can potentially create a lazy, less committed attitude towards the game. If one reconsiders the fact that

"Don't tolerate failure, appreciate it."

50% of the time a hockey player will likely be on a losing team, learning how to take something

positive out of a loss is a valuable quality for all athletes. In a dynamic game like hockey, there are many good plays that intuitive coaches can emphasize even from a poor performance. Unquestionably, coaches must point out mistakes in a calm, objective manner in order to properly teach young hockey players, but focusing on negative parts of the game simply because the team was outscored is not appropriate in minor hockey environments.

RESPECT FOR OPPOSITION AND REFEREES

It has become quite fashionable in minor hockey circles to encourage players to hate their opponents. This kind of attitude is supposed to make them play harder and ultimately lead to more wins. Unfortunately, an attitude of hatred does nothing of the kind. In fact, it creates an environment where retaliation penalties are more prevalent and players lose their composure during the game, decreasing their effectiveness on the ice.

Hockey is not a game for the faint-of-heart—that's a fact. However, an environment of respect for the opposing team need not diminish the intensity of play. Some fans and coaches make the mistake of viewing an injured player on the other team as an opportunity for their team to win rather than what it actually is—an injured child. A more objective observer in the same situation realizes that a young child has been hurt, and that any hatred or aggression that caused the injury should not be tolerated.

As with opposing players, referees often bear the brunt of verbal assaults from players, coaches, and parents. In almost all cases in minor hockey, these are young men and women who are just learning their skills (like the players and the coaches)

and must be given some leeway when it comes to making mistakes. After all, if fans yelled and booed at every player who made a bad play in a game, they would likely be hoarse before the end of the first period! Young referees should be afforded the opportunity to gain their skills in a positive, supportive environment, free from criticism by adults who in most cases are only concerned about one thing—winning!

ENJOYMENT

I am often asked what I consider to be the most important quality that will enable a hockey player to progress to elite levels—university, Olympic, or National Hockey League careers. Is it skating speed, discipline, determination, physical strength? It is true that all of these skills are important components in becoming an effective hockey player. But there is truly only one quality that will determine whether a child even has a chance to progress in this sport, and that is the ability to have fun.

For years I had the privilege of sharing the ice with some of the best players the game has ever seen— Messier, Gretzky, Fuhr, Coffey, and others. I was regularly amazed that although these players were professional athletes and their job was to get back onto the ice each day for games or practices, they all brought with them an undeniable passion for the game they played. Often after practice most of the

players could be found still out on the ice playing three-on-three mini-hockey, or a creative little passing game called "Pig in the Middle." I remember finishing our pregame morning skate at Madison Square Garden in New York. Six or eight of us were at center ice playing "Pig in the Middle," laughing and yelling at the challenge such a simple game provided for us. I looked up at the workers who were busy cleaning the stands in preparation for the upcoming evening event and

> *"In each of us are heroes; speak to them and they will come forth."*
> *–Anonymous*

couldn't help wondering what they were thinking while they watched us. Did they wonder how these professional athletes, pushed every night to perform at their best, could get such innocent pleasure out of the game they played? Since then I have come to the conclusion that likely the main reason why those players became such dominant superstars in the NHL was because they always had so much fun out on the ice!

Coaching Characteristics

Every player who has donned a pair of skates can think of a particular coach who has made a lasting impression in some way. It is hoped that this impression is a positive experience that makes a person's life richer and more fulfilled. Over the years

I have had many coaches, ranging from minor hockey to professional levels. I can remember how each of these men had helped me become the best player I could be. However, one man stood above all others—a man who commanded respect from all his players by his sincerity, commitment, preparedness, consistency, and, above all, his integrity. It is no wonder that this man has become the coach with more wins than any other individual in collegiate hockey: Clare Drake.

> *"A truly great coach continues to give his message to his players even as they sleep."*
> –Randy Gregg

Clare Drake exemplified the best in coaches—he wanted his players to achieve excellence, but winning games was a byproduct of his training, not the main goal. By watching great men like Coach Drake and others, I have tried to analyze the unique characteristics that make these people so special. All coaches should strive to provide positive experiences to all the young hockey players that they coach.

Consider this short list of characteristics that all coaches should strive to be:

1. Be Positive
2. Be in Control
3. Be Prepared
4. Be Consistent
5. Be Fair
6. Be a Teacher
7. Be a Role Model

BE POSITIVE

In the game of hockey there are many opportunities for players to doubt themselves. It is hard for players to be equally skilled in all areas of the game and sometimes their performances may suffer. If that player is in the National Hockey League, he may respond by going into a slump and beginning to second-guess himself. If that player is a minor hockey player, he may respond by quitting hockey and moving on to something else. Neither scenario is desirable, and a coach can help to prevent these occurrences by establishing a positive attitude in the dressing room and on the bench. There is a big difference between quietly correcting mistakes and yelling at a player who errs in the heat of intense play. Both strategies are commonly used in hockey rinks across the country.

Some say that the 1987 Edmonton Oilers team that I had the privilege to play on may have been the most talented hockey team ever assembled. I remember that even with all that talent we still lost 24 games that year. Coaches at the minor hockey level can never guarantee that their team will win every game, and therefore must gauge success not on winning but rather on skill improvement, team progress, and enjoyment. A coach with a positive attitude can always find something good to say about a game or particular player, in order to conclude each event on an uplifting note. Even if the other team scores more goals, I often say, "Never tolerate failure, appreciate it!" Great coaches use losses to teach, motivate, refocus, and prepare their players so that the effort put into playing the game is not wasted.

BE IN CONTROL

Have you ever seen a coach yelling and screaming at the referees or opposition and then turn to one of his players and berate him for losing his temper and taking a bad retaliation penalty? What kind of a mixed message does this give young players? Do they follow their coach's words or his actions? A great coach considers the effects of all his actions and statements long before he initiates them. Staying in control after seeing a blatantly bad call shows the players that the coach has self-discipline and will not lose his focus for the remaining time left in the game. Coaches that motivate by yelling and verbally abusing players and others are quickly ignored. Any effect they have on their players is rapidly lost or shows up later in negative ways. In contrast, coaches who are objective, analytical, and in control of their emotions gain the respect of their players permanently and, as a result, encourage a strong coach/player relationship. Emotional control is a skill that makes stronger teams but also helps to develop this important quality in players who are exposed to it.

BE PREPARED

The coach expects players to be prepared to do their best during every practice and game. Skates in hand with a full set of equipment, the players have intuitively begun preparations for the event long before they hit the ice. In contrast, many coaches come to practice with little forethought of what kind and sequence of drills to use during the ice time and why these particular drills should be run.

A simple practice plan, much like a teacher's lesson plan, is an easy but effective way for coaches to be prepared for and to lead a good practice or game. After all, a player is not much use to a team with only one skate; the same holds true for a coach who does not use the practice ice time effectively or runs an inconsistent bench during a game.

Sample practice plans and a blank templates are available in the Appendix. These sample plans include warmups, drills, and cooldowns that fulfill a specific practice objective. They may be photocopied or adapted for personal use.

BE CONSISTENT

To play the game of hockey proficiently, a young player must master numerous physical and mental skills. This daunting task is made all the more difficult if players are coached inconsistently. Education in schools is based on a specific set of skills, and that curriculum is taught until the particular skills are mastered. This sounds familiar!

Learning in hockey is based on a specific set of skills, including passing, shooting, skating, checking and so on. These are taught repeatedly until the particular skills are mastered. It is crucial that the head coach and assistants understand all the hockey skills and teach them consistently. It is confusing for players to hear two coaches from the same team express completely different opinions on how to play the game. It can make a young player's head spin.

It is important that coaches meet at the beginning of the season to put together a comprehensive plan for team development, including routines for practices and games, skill development, fitness training, and mental preparation. If this kind of long-term planning is done and if goals and routines are established early on, then the players will view the coaching staff as a unit and can begin the process of becoming a team, working together for success.

BE FAIR

One of the most valuable life skills that we as coaches can teach our players is fairness. It is so important to believe that every young athlete on the team is inherently valuable and can contribute to overall success in a variety of ways. The National Hockey League uses role players on each team. These are fellows who may play only once or twice a period. Their job is not to be the goal scorer, rather just to fill an important

space on a team that needs both superstars and grinders. Unfortunately, many inexperienced coaches see this strategy in the professional ranks and believe it should also be used in minor hockey.

There is only one reason why coaches preferentially play their best players and allow their less skilled players to sit out more frequently. That is to win, of course! There is nothing inherently wrong with trying to win games. In fact, part of the challenge of games like hockey is to be able to rate oneself and one's team against the opposition. Unfortunately, many coaches overlook the price that is paid for trying to win at all costs. Imagine how devastating it must feel when a player's biggest role model in hockey, the coach, tells him to miss the next shift in order to put a better player out there instead. These seemingly inconsequential occurrences during a game are hardly remembered by the coach, but the effect on the player can be profound.

The solution is simple. Great coaches in minor hockey systems play all players equally. They teach their players to lose as a team. They teach them to win as a team. The notion of team building is a powerful concept, not only in sport but also as a legacy for school, family, and business experiences in the future.

BE A TEACHER

There are many roles that a coach must assume in minor hockey, including skate tightener, bus driver, and friend. A coach must be able to run efficient practices and be able to control the flow of player changes during games. By far the most important role of a coach is to be a teacher.

Every young player deserves the opportunity to learn the proper hockey skills in a positive and enriching environment. In addition, invaluable personal qualities such as self-esteem, discipline, anger control, respect for opponents, and being able to win and lose like champions can be taught to all hockey participants. When I am behind the bench or on the ice with my young players, I try to think of myself first as a teacher, second as a coach!

BE A ROLE MODEL

The highest compliment any hockey coach can receive is when a player comes back ten years after playing on the team and says how fondly he remembers his hockey experience that year. In most cases players cannot even remember whether they won more games than they lost, but great hockey seasons are based on experiences much more important than simply winning or losing.

It is often said that a loss is only a loss if you don't learn anything from it! Great coaches can turn the worst season's record into a positive experience not soon forgotten by all players. To do so coaches must become leaders, role models for every player on the team. If coaches show discipline, integrity, and goodwill that we as parents hope our children will someday possess, then that goal becomes more easily attainable. Coaches are much like a mother duck followed by a brood of baby ducklings. If led to scream, blame, hate, and be undisciplined, then the players will unhesitatingly follow. But if the coach leads by creating a spirit of camaraderie and fair play, respect for referees and opposition, winning and losing with honor and dignity, using hockey to have fun, then amazing things happen to the players involved!

Practice Organization

Many hockey experts believe a game is the worst place for a coach to teach new skills to players. The tempo of the game is fast and both players and coaching staff are usually preoccupied with the flow of the game, thus making learning new skills difficult. For this reason, good coaches use their practice time as effectively as possible in order to develop their players' skills in an atmosphere of learning and acceptance.

What sorts of things can a coach do to make practices most effective? Consider the following:

1. Have a plan.
2. Follow a consistent drill sequence.
3. Slowly integrate more advanced drills.

HAVE A PLAN

Before every practice and game, all coaches ask their players to be ready with equipment and skates on, stick taped, and minds focused on hockey. These same players have a fundamental right as well to have their coach prepared to run a well-organized, enjoyable, yet demanding practice. There is nothing more wasteful than seeing a coach show up ten minutes before practice with absolutely no idea what they will do on the ice. Often these practices turn into scrimmage sessions, which of course the players love but unfortunately do little to teach them any of the fundamental skills of the game.

Great coaches always write down an outline or plan for every practice that they run. Much like teachers who develop a lesson plan for each subject on each day, coaches can easily spend a few minutes prior to leaving for the rink to put some ideas down on paper. Not only does it organize one's thoughts about the team and where some of their weaknesses lie, it shows all the players that the coach is committed to helping the team become the best it can. Even if a coach is too rushed and cannot make a new practice plan, keeping a stock of old practice plans in a binder is a simple way of being organized. The Appendix contains sample practice plans to accomplish specific practice objectives and a blank template that can be photocopied and/or modified for personal use.

FOLLOW A CONSISTENT DRILL SEQUENCE

Mastering the skills of any dynamic game takes constant repetition during practice and improving execution during game situations. It therefore makes good sense to organize practices in a way that players of all ages can develop a rhythm of learning that simplifies the sometimes-difficult task of acquiring new skills.

It is not uncommon for experienced coaches to establish a template for practices. They begin with a stretching and warmup drill, followed by a skating drill that may emphasize agility, speed, or power. Following the natural progression of hockey skills, drills would then incorporate individual puckhandling, passing, and shooting skills. Midway through the practice, the coach may schedule drills that work on team concepts: forechecking systems, breakouts, power plays, and penalty killing. To end the practice, the coach may run the players through skating drills aimed at improving conditioning. If a coach follows such a progression of drills, the players soon begin

After retiring from the National Hockey League, I was privileged to coach my young sons in a very introductory level of minor hockey. Of course, when starting out we had to work mainly on skating skills, but it wasn't long before these young players were doing the same drills that I had done for years with the Edmonton Oilers. The kids obviously didn't perform them at a high level and I had to simplify the drills a lot to make them easier to understand, but the same drill concept applied. As I followed my boys to higher levels of minor hockey, the drills remained constant, with the only changes being more technical variations added, as the players became ready for them. My sons and their group of friends have been exposed to similar practice drills for three to four years consecutively! It is enjoyable to see how easy practice has become for them simply because they are comfortable with this consistent practice organization and drill progression.

to feel more comfortable with the flow of the practice sessions. Improved performance is likely. Making better hockey players by following a consistent practice drill sequence is assured.

Note: Coaches should consider saving their conditioning skating drills until the end of practice for a number of reasons. The players tend to have more energy for the skill-related drills in the middle of the practice and a higher practice tempo is usually established. In addition, the ice surface is not damaged by hard skating early in practice, so stickhandling, passing, and shooting drills can be performed on a much better quality of ice.

SLOWLY INTEGRATE MORE ADVANCED DRILLS

Much like a teacher in a school, hockey coaches must progressively stimulate their players to ensure that their skills continue to improve. Once a team has mastered a particular drill, experienced coaches add a slight technical variation or insert a more advanced drill in order to challenge the players at a higher level. Good practice drills are those that simulate game situations closely, and with the dynamic and exciting nature of the game of hockey, coaches can easily develop a series of drill progressions that can be used from novice to professional levels!

A Final Word about Attitude

A great coach can teach players that the whole point of playing is not simply to win. Winning is such a limiting goal for an experience that can be so much more worthwhile. It is the coach's responsibility to ensure that all players leave their hockey encounter with something more than just the satisfaction of winning. The game provides the the teacher/coach many important opportunities

• to develop technical skills,

• to improve the fitness levels of a group of interested individuals, and

• to teach important life skills such as self-esteem, self-confidence, and discipline.

What an awesome responsibility! Responsible coaches realize that they have a tremendous influence over a group of impressionable bodies and minds, and that this influence endures long after the athletes leave their care. It is a coach's responsibility to ensure that not only do their players leave more skilled, but that they also leave better people with their self-esteem and confidence intact and a positive outlook that will carry them through life.

Chapter 9

10 - Mental Preparation

It is ironic that, in the past, hockey coaches, parents, and players have focused their attention solely on the technical aspect of hockey development. Each year teams seem to be doing more and more fund raising to provide additional ice time so that their players will have ample time to master hockey skills. Recently, however, amateur hockey groups are following the lead of other sporting groups (including elite college and national hockey programs) and have begun incorporating physical conditioning that includes dryland training as a significant component in the development of hockey players. This acceptance of physical conditioning will undoubtedly help to develop stronger, more skilled, and talented players.

There is a third component of athletic development, however, and that is mental preparation. Many coaches and athletes who have reached elite levels in sport understand how mental preparation can significantly influence athletic performance. Olympic and national level athletes use mental preparation techniques as a valuable tool to improve their chances of success. The sport of hockey has been slow to adopt this important initiative, except at the higher levels of professional, collegiate, and national hockey. Mental preparation

> *"When we quiet the mind, the symphony begins."*
> *–Anonymous*

can make the difference between success and failure, and players of all ages can benefit from learning techniques to enhance their performance. For minor hockey players, there are simple techniques that will help youngsters increase the likelihood of achieving their potential as athletes. This section outlines some of these techniques and provides suggestions on how to use them.

After watching great players for many years, I concluded that their mental keenness came as naturally as their intelligence, size, and hair color. Unfortunately, not everyone can have the natural mental grounding of a Gretzky or a Messier and many of these skills cannot be taught directly. However, it is where a coach's modeling of behaviors and a coach's approach to teaching and learning play an important role. This is where great coaches can use drill organization, personal interaction with players, and their general philosophy toward the game to develop their players' mental strength—a collection of important skills that will stay with players for a lifetime.

MENTAL PREPARATION FOR HOCKEY PLAYERS

Hundreds of books advocate the importance of mental training for athletes and suggest ways that coaches can enhance this learning process. After reading many of these books, however, I often came away without clear understanding of the steps that I could take as a coach to instruct players in mental preparation techniques. Using the work of experienced sport psychologists and my personal experience at various levels of hockey, I have developed and feel comfortable with a simplified concept of mental preparation for minor hockey participants. This approach may help coaches to

It was when I first played for Canada's Olympic Team in 1980 that I was exposed to techniques of mental training by sport psychologists. Since I did not feel that I had an abundance of physical talent, I was quite excited to learn more about the ways that I could gain any advantage over the opposition. I read as many books as I could on the subject and tried to develop a mental strategy that worked best for me. As my career took me to the National Hockey League and the Edmonton Oilers, I watched how my teammates used mental training to their advantage—especially the great ones like Gretzky and Messier—and tried to discover their secrets of success.

These players were great athletes with excellent physical strength, power, speed, and endurance. Like me, they had learned their skills in a minor hockey system, though some would say that those skills were enhanced by all the outdoor hockey they played as youngsters, something that is not as common now. However, it was more difficult to detect how they achieved the inner strength necessary to become superstars. They had confidence, a heightened self-esteem, the amazing ability to focus mentally, a great attitude toward the game, and an unparalleled work ethic. However, none of these players had worked with a sport psychologist or had taken specialized training in using the mental component of hockey to their advantage. Inner strength comes naturally to some players which is likely one of the main reasons these particular fellows became dominant players in the game.

understand the valuable ideas and tactics that can be used to develop the complete hockey player.

I have divided mental training into three major areas:

1. Thinking
2. Believing
3. Responding

Under each of these three areas I have listed several components that contribute to the specific aspect of mental training with suggestions for incorporating them into practices and games.

Thinking

This is the rational part of mental preparation. It deals with positive attitude toward self and the game, development of the intuitive aspect of play, and just plain having fun while playing the game. These are the factors of mental training that players can logically consider, reason through, and learn to use if they have enough practice and reinforcement.

POSITIVE ATTITUDE

Most coaches have come across a player who although blessed with a wealth of physical talent has a negative self-image and a poor attitude toward others. This player constantly looks for the negative side of events and never seems to enjoy or share in the exciting moments of hockey. This attitude may sometimes stem from an unstable family situation, illness, poor grades at school, negative interactions with teammates, or just a difficult stage of adolescence. Unfortunately, players like these not only undermine their own potential significantly, but also adversely affect their teammates. In these cases it is essential that the coach make every effort to counteract this negative attitude.

> *"It is not true that nice guys finish last; nice guys are winners before the game even starts."*
> *—Addison Walker*

What can a coach do to ensure that players come to the rink with a positive attitude and maintain that attitude through losses, teasing from teammates, and the struggle to learn new skills? Since a coach generally only sees a group of players for a few hours a week during practices and games, it is virtually impossible to address concerns of family, health, or academic struggles. However, a coach can work to develop a strong team environment in the dressing room and on the bench that will provide all players with a sense of unity and team commitment. Working together to reach a common goal may help a young player who is struggling psychologically to overcome the feelings of bitterness and frustration that lead to a negative attitude.

Coaches are important role models for players and can lead by the example of their own attitudes. If a coach consistently complains or reacts negatively to situations on the ice, then that coach must expect the same from the players. Conversely, if the coach tries to approach every situation—good or bad—in a positive frame of mind, then the players are more likely to imitate these actions and attitudes.

Positive reinforcement is also a powerful tool for motivating young athletes. Reinforcing a positive attitude by commending players or rewarding them with some form of team recognition is a valuable way of turning players away from negativity and toward being a positive force and an integral part of a team.

For instance, in a situation where a player consistently displays a poor or selfish attitude, a coach can look carefully for important teaching

When I played for the Edmonton Oilers, the equipment manager was a man named Barrie Stafford. He was a former player with the University of Alberta Golden Bears who had the heart and desire of a superstar but unfortunately was without a matching level of physical talent. That did not stop Barrie from becoming a valuable part of our Stanley Cup winning teams. Barrie used to say, "There are never any problems in life, only opportunities!"

It is a simple statement but it speaks volumes when considering players' attitudes. A coach with a positive attitude can turn the problem of a bad play into a teaching opportunity. A coach with a positive attitude can turn the problem of a lost game into the opportunity of learning from that loss. A coach with a positive attitude can also turn a player with a negative attitude into a positive contributor! All of this can be accomplished with a few simple words of encouragement to the team or to individuals.

opportunities. Over the course of a game, every player invariably does something to help the team, whether it is blocking a shot, making a strong backchecking effort, or taking a hard hit to make a nice pass. A good coach can use these opportunities to recognize the player's efforts in front of the teammates, identifying that it is these qualities that are necessary to form a strong team bond. If coaches are consistent in these efforts, then they can develop the team concept of unselfish play and heightened camaraderie.

INTUITION

There are hundreds of thousands of hockey players in the world who learn a similar set of skills in order to become the best players they can be. Many will be fortunate to have qualified coaches and adequate ice time in order to develop their skills enough to be selected to play at an elite level. Only a few, however, will develop that special awareness that sets great players apart from all the rest. Intuition is the ability to predict situations on the ice before they happen and to react instinctively to improve performance. The best players have this uncanny insight that enables them to prepare for certain situations long before others see them. Gretzky, Bourque, and Lemeiux are three players who have that special intuition that makes playing hockey truly an art form.

How can hockey coaches work on developing intuitive players? It is not an easy task. Many young players simply do not have the ability to develop such keenness towards the game. However, a coach can vary the practice drills, changing them constantly to prevent players from becoming mentally stale. It is too easy for a coach to repeat drills until the players not only master the skill but become so relaxed that they do not put maximum effort and thought into the drill. Constant repetition provides little challenge  for the players to creatively predict and respond to a wide variety of on-ice situations.

Many experts believe that this game-related insight demonstrated by the great ones was honed through many hours of nonstructured play on the outdoor rinks when these players were young. Without the formal game structure, coaches, practice drills, and score boards, these youngsters had the opportunity to take chances, try new skills, and try to predict the flow of the outdoor shinny game without the controls imposed by hockey organizations. Intuition is a valuable skill for hockey players at all levels, but may be one that a coach has only a minor part in helping to develop.

I use dryland games with my players to promote the development of intuitive minds. "Aeroball" is a game similar to team handball. It can easily be organized in a gymnasium or community hall. Players are divided into two teams. Two sets of pylons are arranged at both ends of the gym. The game is played with a soft ball. The object is to score a point by either running through the opposing goal or by successfully passing the ball through the goal to a teammate. Defenders gain possession of the ball by touching the opposing player who is carrying the ball. The object of "Aeroball" therefore is to advance the ball forward by breaking into openings and passing the ball quickly between teammates while eluding opposing players. It is amazing the speed, anticipation, and creativity that develop after only a few games!

> While playing with the Oilers, parents would often ask us what summer activity was best to help their son or daughter become a better hockey player. In most cases we suggested, baseball, lacrosse, or swimming. There are many alternatives to summer hockey that challenge children to improve their balance, coordination, conditioning, agility, and power, yet not burn them out mentally prior to the start of the next season.

Although not played on skates, the game helps hockey players improve many of the skills needed to become successful athletes, not the least of which is intuition.

ENJOYMENT

Having fun by participating in an activity is a simple concept but cannot be emphasized enough. Yet in the sport of hockey some parents and coaches have become somewhat misguided in their notions of how their children must think about the game. Some think that since hockey is a fast-paced physical game, players should be challenged and forced to perform with maximal effort at all times. Promoting skating drills that are repeated until the players drop from exhaustion or constantly reprimanding players for subpar efforts, these parents and coaches believe

that hard work, perspiration, and striving to win are more important than enjoying the game. Unfortunately for the players who must endure this military-style approach to a sporting activity, they are often pushed into retiring from the game long before they deserve to or even wish to.

It is a fallacy that, if players are having fun, then they must not be working hard and therefore they are wasting their time on the ice. On the contrary, fun practice drills and a positive coaching environment encourages players to deliver maximal effort and also contributes to a lifelong love of the game and sporting activity in general. Because few hockey players will actually make a living from the game, the reward for the vast majority must come from the thrill of participating, being part of a team, and having a great time on the ice.

Two simple guidelines can help a coach ensure that the players enjoy their hockey experience:

1. Begin with constructive suggestions and end with positive reinforcement. If a coach must be critical of a player's or the team's performance, then it is important to point out or discuss the problem early in practice so that it can be worked on during the practice drills. Then at the end of the practice, it is important that the coach finishes with a positive statement or observation. Since he may not see these players for several days, he wants them to be thinking positively about their hockey during their time off rather than continually being reminded of a negative experience.

Constructive suggestions followed by drills specifically designed to remedy problems early on in a practice coupled with positive comments at the end of practice produce enthusiastic hockey players who are committed to the team effort and willing to give their best at practices and games!

2. Incorporate a fun game to finish off the practice. It could be three-on-three mini-hockey at each end of the rink, a shootout, or other fun competition. The enjoyable experience at the end of practice leaves players in a positive frame of mind between practices and brings each one back the next time with a positive attitude and an energetic approach to the game.

A good example of an effective closing drill for practice is the shootout. Each player gets an opportunity to try a breakaway on the goaltenders at both ends of the rink. Coaches can encourage each player to skate quickly towards the net and try a variety of breakaway moves. Although the odds of scoring on both goalies is small even for the best players on the team, most will leave the ice with a positive feeling of excitement rather than a negative feeling of frustration or criticism.

Although not every coach or parent agrees with this philosophy of sport, having fun is the single most important factor in determining whether youngsters continue to play this glorious game!

Believing

This is the emotional part of mental preparation. It includes enhancing a player's self-image, promoting a positive direction for a player's hockey experience, and teaching players the ability to focus mentally and ignore outside distractions. Fear of failure, lack of confidence in their own abilities, and being easily distracted can significantly affect players' performances. However, there are strategies that coaches can use to help players gain a better self-image, have a positive direction and be able to focus on the task at hand amid many distractions. Some of these strategies are included in this section.

ENHANCED SELF-IMAGE

Many hockey players have become successful not necessarily because of their talent, but rather because of a confidence in their abilities. There are many more role players on a hockey team than there are superstars, yet if they all became frustrated because they could not score all the goals, then they would likely consider their hockey experience to be a failure. Belief in oneself and in one's ability to perform is possibly the most important quality that an athlete can possess. Without a strong self-image, players often spend valuable energy questioning themselves and their abilities rather than gaining confidence in learning new skills and in perfecting known skills. Gaining the confidence to perform at an optimal level not only produces good hockey players but can also provide direction and encouragement for these same children at school, in the family setting, and with future career choices.

What can coaches do to enhance their players' self-image through hockey?

1. Develop a positive approach towards teaching players new skills.

Every minor hockey player must learn a multitude of skills and concepts at every level. None are so skilled or so clever that they perform perfectly at all times, nor are any likely to perform a new skill perfectly the first time it is taught. Indeed, not even the greatest players ever to play the game can say that they have never made a mistake.

There are two ways a coach can give feedback to a player who has made an error—positively or negatively. Both of these forms of reinforcement give the player information on the mistake, but the effect of each on the player's self-image is vastly different. Negative reinforcement can destroy a player's confidence in his abilities and often leads to a closed-minded player who becomes afraid to fail in situations both on and off the ice. Calling someone "stupid" or complaining about a mistake that let the team down can alienate a young player from any sport. Players consistently exposed to negative reinforcement often tend to shy away from new challenges because the pain of failure has become stronger than the excitement of success.

As an example, a coach who sees a player intercept an opposing pass and then give it right back to the other team can focus his initial comments on the good anticipation and skill of the pass interception, followed by a less aggressive comment regarding the poor decision shortly after. The young player will respond to this form of reinforcement by looking forward to making a great play next time instead of becoming afraid of making another mistake. A team who loses a game in overtime can still be commended for their hard effort during the game. Young players will develop an attitude that, in tight situations, they have nothing to be afraid of and can go out and give their best effort every game.

> *"Then the time came when the risk it took to remain tight in bud was more painful that the risk it took to blossom."*
> *–Anais Nin*

Coaches who use positive reinforcement can still inform players of mistakes but they give players a chance to respond more positively and, as a result, players are more apt to try harder and play smarter the next time. This technique is a great way to keep young players improving consistently.

2. Allow athletes to evaluate their play. A valuable technique for coaches to teach the skills of hockey to young players is to turn the tables and allow the athletes to evaluate how they have performed in various game situations. Coaches can ask the players what they think they did wrong on the play rather than telling them. This form of dialogue produces thinking, intuitive players who each year become even easier to coach. They can become their own coaches, able to analyze situations and make changes without any input from adult coaches! One potential drawback, though, is that some

players might begin trying to analyze the mistakes of their teammates. The head coach has to be aware that this reaction can break down the spirit of a team as quickly as empowering the players can build it up and be ready to intervene in what could become a volatile situation.

After making a poor decision on passing the puck out of the defensive zone, a coach may elect to say, "What do you think would be a better decision on that pass?" rather than "You've got to make a smarter pass in our zone." The young player has the opportunity to analyze the play and come up with a good option for the next time that situation presents itself. Players become thinkers, not just reactors.

> *"Remember, no one can make you feel inferior without your consent."*
> *—Eleanor Roosevelt*

POSITIVE DIRECTION

A common saying is, "You never see a bad winner, just bad losers." Indeed, it is much easier to be a winning coach or a member of a winning hockey team. The Oilers teams that I played on were fortunate to win five Stanley Cups in the eight years I was with the team. Even with this amazing championship record, those teams still lost several games during the season and did not win the Cup in three of the eight years.

If the players had reacted to each loss with frustration and anger, we may never have won any of those Stanley Cups. On the contrary, those great players responded to a losing streak with an even more determined outlook for the next game or season, vowing to learn from their mistakes and become better in the future.

Losing is a part of the game, whether it is the result of a one-on-one in the corner of the rink or a loss on the scoreboard. It takes a thoughtful and perceptive coach to turn that loss in the corner or on the scoreboard into a positive learning experience. By role modeling a positive attitude and by treating all players as valued team members, coaches can help players develop an attitude that sees beyond the statistics of wins and losses, good plays and bad plays. Those coaches focus on a positive future direction for both individuals and the team. Instead of being frustrated by a bad play, their players learn to have a positive direction, increase their intensity, and work harder. They do not take retaliation penalties because they understand how an unnecessary infraction could ultimately hurt their team. They understand that retaliation represents a loss of self-control. Athletes who are able to handle difficult situations on the ice without losing their temper or making poor decisions are a coach's dream and will some day reach their ultimate hockey playing potential. More importantly, however, they will also likely be successful in other areas of their lives, whether in their families, in their education, or at their jobs.

> *"The most important thing is not to win, but to take part, just as the most important thing in life is not the triumph, but the attempt. The essential thing is not to have conquered, but to have fought well."*
> –Olympic Creed 1894

Fear of failure can become a major stumbling block for many elite athletes. It is natural for a coach to use a poor play or mistake to correct a player or make suggestions for improvement during a practice or a game. However, if a correction

THE TECHNICAL, THE PHYSICAL, AND THE MENTAL GAME

is made in a negative or demeaning way, the player may begin to feel uncomfortable with any form of criticism. Soon worrying about making a mistake can seem more important than making a great play. The outside negative reinforcement becomes internalized and the result can be devastating to the confidence of young players. It often leads to them dropping out of organized hockey. So it is essential that coaches are sensitive to how their criticism is perceived by players and that players are comfortable with the on-ice learning process where suggestions for improvement are taken in the spirit of learning rather than in an atmosphere of negativity. Promoting a positive direction in a young hockey player's mind takes a careful balance of constructive criticism and enthusiastic encouragement!

> *Promoting a positive direction in a young hockey player's mind takes a careful balance of constructive criticism and enthusiastic encouragement!*

Early in the year I tell my players that they should not be worried about making mistakes during practice, because that is the best time for experimentation, risk-taking, and learning. I would much rather they make a mistake in practice than in the middle of an important game! In fact, I emphasize that making a mistake while trying their best, whether in a practice or game, shows that they are trying to become the best players possible. This discussion, held several times early in the year, tends to allow players to feel more comfortable with practice errors and, as a result, they are more open to trying new skills, techniques, and tactics. The nice carryover into game situations is that the players become accustomed to more readily accepting suggestions for improvement.

Young hockey players can develop a positive mental attitude toward learning by having a coach who has an accepting approach to mistakes on the ice and who uses them in a positive way to help a player improve skills. Consistency is key, however, as a coach must learn to deal positively with mistakes that may cost a win in an important game in just the same way as an error can during practice. This is not an easy task, but experience and commitment to an optimal learning environment for all hockey players must be the primary goal.

MENTAL FOCUS

As much as hockey is a fast-paced, dynamic game, it is also one where there are many distractions. Players can get caught up with individual battles against opposing players, concerns of a perceived lack of playing time or personality conflicts with teammates. Having a strong mental focus allows a player to deal with distractions without losing the mental intensity for the task at hand. This part outlines

OMMMMM··

techniques, such as visualization, for helping players to achieve that focus and to help them filter out the many distractions that threaten their concentration during a game. Consider these techniques:

1. Entering "the zone." Achieving a strong mental focus has often been called entering "the zone." It is a place where athletes can seemingly block out all extraneous pressures in order to perform at an optimal level. Successful golfers have

While I was playing in the National Hockey League, games held in cities like New York or Philadelphia were as much fun as playing at home. These fans were rabid supporters of the Rangers or the Flyers and were often so noisy that it was hard for the players to hear anything else. We were not distracted, however, because we had learned to focus our total attention on the game and to block out extraneous noise. In fact, we were often not even aware that fans were yelling because we were so focused on the plays and strategy of the game. I must admit that it was far more difficult to stay focused when the fans in those cities began to throw things at us. It is hoped that minor hockey players do not have to worry about that!

the uncanny knack of losing themselves in concentration so that not even the exhilaration of sinking a challenging putt affects their continued performance. Professional basketball players can shut out the screaming fans while focusing on an all-important free throw.

Unfortunately in minor hockey, young players often give in to frustration and swing their sticks in disgust after missing an open net, smash them against the boards after making bad plays, or loudly and derisively challenge referees' calls. The coach's role in situations such as these is to consistently reinforce that these actions are detrimental to the team and the player individually. Coaches must demonstrate how a secure mental focus allows the athlete to disregard past events and to refocus on the plays coming up during the rest of the game. This is a difficult concept for young players so learning how to "enter the zone" early on and practicing doing so will transform a simply competent player into one who consistently rises above any frustration.

2. Visualization. To enhance mental focus, elite athletes all over the world use the practice of **visualization**. Ski racers race the course in their minds many times before a competition. Lugists, bob sledders, figure skaters, gymnasts, divers, and other athletes use visualization techniques to refine their mental focus long before competition begins.

For athletes unfamiliar with visualization techniques, it is simply the process of seeing in the mind's eye all the elements of a successful performance without actually physically executing the movements. For example, a winger might, early on game day, close his eyes and repetitively picture how he might approach a breakaway. He sees in his mind how fast he will skate, what the goalie may do with his glove and blocker while backing into the net, whether he will use a forehand or a backhand

Visualization

shot, and finally he watches as his shot goes deep into the net for a goal. Repetitive visualization of successful events can instill a sense of confidence in players so that they feel more comfortable when the situation actually arises during a game. Visualization costs nothing in terms of ice time rental; it is not stressful to the body; and, when done in a positive context, can be an important component in the mental preparation of a hockey athlete.

Coaches of young hockey players can easily teach their athletes the art of visualization. A coach can make this exercise fun for all players so that they begin to feel more comfortable with a mental approach that is initially foreign to them. Visualization practice is as simple as asking all players before practice to close their eyes and think of a particular situation that may happen on the ice, say a breakaway. Ask the players to follow the play in their minds, focusing on all the details, such as how their skates are moving, where their hands are positioned on their sticks, and their breathing rate. Make sure that they finish off their visualized play with a positive outcome, such as a goal. Goaltenders can finish their visualization with a great glove save or a timely poke check that prevents scoring. A coach can develop a variety of visualization experiences for the players during the season, all related to an important play or one that occurs frequently during a game.

> *"Obstacles are those frightful things we see when we take our eyes off the goal."*
> *–Hanah More*

Visualization Examples

1. *Forward skating down the ice on a breakaway*
2. *Goaltender reacting to a breakaway*
3. *Defenseman playing a one-on-one from the corner*
4. *Forward attempting an offensive play out of the corner*
5. *Center controlling the puck behind the offensive goal*

The players may or may not choose to continue this visualization process on their own, but at least their coach has introduced a skill to them that may become a very important tool in their futures.

Responding

This is the reacting part of mental preparation. It is the result of all of a player's prior work and training. It includes discipline, work ethic, and learning interest. Ultimate success in hockey, or in any life endeavor, is often more the result of hard work than anything else. This section describes skills and strategies for teaching young players to play smart hockey. These are strategies that coaches cannot teach directly, but they are those that can be encouraged and promoted with a focus on why most kids really want to play hockey—to have fun with their friends.

It is human nature to want to learn and to seek new skills, even though children sometimes give the impression that learning is the last thing they wish to do. However, when an activity is fun and progressively challenges their skill level, then they will work at it until they have mastered the skill or concept. All three mental skills discussed in this section— thinking, believing, responding—come from

within and cannot be imposed or taught directly. They are a result of watching adult behavior and modeling it. They can be developed in children, but only with encouragement and a coaching philosophy that incorporates and promotes the positive attitudes discussed in Chapter 9, "Attitudes in Hockey."

DISCIPLINE

Discipline is defined as the systematic training, exercise, development, and control of one's mental, moral, and physical faculties. Often overheard in arenas across the country is a comment about how one particular player is showing so much discipline in a game situation. In contrast, every elite sport has its examples of athletes with amazing physical talent who have reacted negatively to a mistake, an unlucky play, or an official's decision. When players let frustrations get the better of them, they lose mental focus and intensity of play for minutes or occasionally for the rest of the game or tournament.

During every professional golf tournament across the country there are examples of elite athletes

losing mental focus after rimming out a putt or landing in a bunker. The viewers watch that athlete's game fall apart with one bad shot after another. A goaltender who has trouble refocusing mentally after a weak goal often lets in two or three more in rapid succession simply because of a lack of mental discipline. In some cases these mental lapses can mean the difference between a championship effort and a poor performance.

Retaliating with a two-handed swing of the stick after being on the receiving end of a solid check is an example of a lack of discipline that can hurt both player and team. The resulting penalty gives the other team a power play and possibly an important goal. Unfortunately however, in some hockey circles, retaliation is thought to be a sign of toughness or sticking up for oneself or a teammate, by being unwilling to passively accept a physical blow. Some coaches even applaud such actions, suggesting that the player is displaying toughness or aggression.

However, as the game of hockey evolves in tactics and training, most coaches have come to realize that this eye-for-an-eye attitude is detrimental because it reinforces the notion that players should feel comfortable hitting their opposition but should never allow the same to be done to them. It also reinforces a lack of respect for the referee's authority and allows players to think that they can enforce the rules of the game as they see fit. A coach who has a positive attitude and who demands discipline from the players uses these situations to teach the team that a player who takes a hit and skates away is the one who is truly tough. Having the discipline to keep emotions in check while at the same time possibly helping the team by bringing about a power play situation shows who is really in control.

> *"How we play the game reveals something of our character; how we lose shows all of it."*
> *–Anonymous*

A common example of lack of discipline is when a player or coach complains to the referee about an offside call, a penalty call, a disallowed goal, or other judgmental decision. These complaints are often directed at young referees who are gaining valuable on-ice experience. Referees certainly make mistakes in both judgement and skill; however, they should not have to take verbal abuse for their errors. In all the years of playing both as an amateur and a professional, I have never seen a referee change a call simply because of a complaint by a coach or a player. In fact, complaints can often anger a referee and there is a chance that he may hold a grudge against the complaining team for the rest of the game, calling more penalties than he may otherwise have called. Holding grudges is not appropriate behavior for referees since they are encouraged to remain neutral, not favoring one team over another. However, many minor hockey officials have not gained the maturity or experience to be perfectly impartial. When I am coaching I deliberately stay quiet even after a blatantly bad call to model the behavior that I expect from my team and so that they can see that losing control is not at all productive.

Discipline is a life skill that helps a person decide on a plan of action and stick to the plan despite distractions. The game of hockey is a perfect environment to nurture this valuable life skill. Young players cannot become truly great without understanding the importance of a disciplined approach to the game. Similarly, businessmen, teachers, musicians, and virtually every worker cannot fulfill his or her ultimate potential without a disciplined approach to work. As a hockey coach, the first step to teaching discipline to young players is to model a consistently disciplined attitude during practices and games. Losing one's temper on the bench, throwing water bottles, and yelling at the referees are examples of how coaches can show players what not to do! Accepting judgment calls even if they go against the team, controlling emotions behind the bench during games, and working hard at being prepared for practices are great ways to instill in your team the concept of mental discipline.

> *"Everyone has a talent; but rare is the courage to follow the talent to the places it leads."*
> *–Erica Jong*

WORK ETHIC

Considering the fact that development of the total hockey player requires a combination of technical, physical, and mental training, it goes without saying that success requires a great deal of hard work. For some young players, the notion of working hard is foreign because they have never had to push themselves in any sport or physical activity. Hockey can be the perfect training ground for young athletes, because learning the importance of hard work is directly associated with a playing atmosphere that is fun and exciting.

What strategies can a coach use to help develop a strong work ethic in players?

1. Run well-organized practices. Organization is one of the most important ways to develop a strong work ethic. The section on practice organization in Chapter 9, "Attitudes in Hockey" can be a valuable tool for designing a practice plan that is effective in developing, not only skills, but a sense of how to work to best achieve success with those skills. If players stand around a lot during practice, watching others more than skating themselves, they tend to become accustomed to a lower ratio of work  to rest. As a result, when those players are pushed to skate hard for longer periods of time in a game, they do not have the stamina or mental intensity to maintain a high level of play. The key is to plan a practice with minimal downtime for players so that they develop consistently strong work habits and stamina, both of which transfer well to game situations.

Many of the greatest coaches that I played under rarely extended practice beyond sixty or seventy-five minutes. Their thinking was that by keeping practices shorter but well organized, the players could perform drills at a higher tempo, thus developing higher skill levels and establishing a stronger work ethic. There was little standing around during these practices and, at the end, every player was exhausted. Compare this position with that of the coach who schedules a two-hour practice with many rest periods to discuss strategy or the technical aspects of the game. Most players naturally hold back the intensity of their play in order to make it through the whole practice and these rest periods greatly increase the rest-to-work ratio. Consider the efficiency and effectiveness of using the time before practice to discuss strategy, thus reserving ice time for high intensity training.

2. Make practice fun! Many coaches believe that players must work as hard as they can to benefit the most from practice. I certainly agree with that. Yet it is indisputable that players will naturally work harder in practice because they want to, rather than because they have to. Any coach can blow a whistle and force players to skate around the rink. A great coach can get the same or better practice intensity when players are having fun and the drills are challenging and exciting. Incorporating games that work important individual skills like skating speed, agility, and power is a perfect way to ensure 100% intensity. See Chapter 2, "Individual Skills" for a selection of games and drills that will assist in building individual and team skills.

> *The most important way to ensure the development of a strong work ethic is to make practice fun!*

3. Finish every practice with a set of closing remarks. This is a time, at the conclusion of all the drills, when the head coach summarizes how practice went. It is a crucial time for coaches to be positive because it may be the last interaction they will have with the players for several days. If coaches conclude practices in a negative, angry manner, then the players have many days to remember that impression and embellish it. However, if practice ends on a positive, upbeat note, then players have those days to remember how much fun hockey is. To recap, work ethic develops when players work hard because they want to, not because they have to!

It is unrealistic to think that every hockey team is comprised only of players who work hard every drill and throughout their game shifts. Invariably coaches have lazy, less-motivated players who are hesitant or even unable to give 100% effort at all times simply because they do not know how. A good philosophy for coaches in situations like this is not to give up on any particular player, but rather to ensure that each player ends the season with an enhanced sense of work ethic compared to when they began tryouts or practices.

Success in coaching is measured on many levels when dealing with the diverse group of individuals that make up a hockey team. That is why consistent modeling of expected behaviors and promoting a good work ethic through fun, exciting drills is so important to the success of any coach at any level of minor hockey.

LEARNING INTEREST

It is possible to teach every youngster how to play hockey, but it is much more difficult to teach him or her to play smart hockey! Of the thousands of hockey players at every age level who are good skaters, puckhandlers, and shooters, what makes the difference between the great ones and all the rest? For many years during training camp in the National Hockey League, I saw many young players come straight out of junior hockey ready to set the world on fire. They had good skills, they could shoot the puck, and they were fast on their skates. It only took about two days to see that these players had no chance of making the big squad. It became obvious that they had reached the junior level simply because of their skills and not because of their smarts. When they were challenged with new and more intricate drills, they would often become frustrated because they were not able to comprehend or perform them easily. Hockey had come easy to these players because of their size, skill, and determination. Unfortunately, in many cases, they had not been challenged to continue learning the more intricate fundamentals of the game. Being excited about learning and understanding how strongly this correlates with success, whether in hockey, at school, or in business, is an integral step to reaching optimal performance.

> *"Unless we try to do something beyond what we have already mastered, we cannot grow."*
> *–Ronald Osborn*

What can a coach do to stimulate learning interest in all the players on the team? Using and refining drills that constantly require a player to assess a situation and react accordingly challenges them to become smarter hockey players. Drills that are boring and repetitive may help to develop technical hockey skills; unfortunately, these also tend to elicit automated responses from players, definitely not a habit that coaches want to reinforce in their players. Using drills that become progressively more complicated challenge players and teach them both physical and mental skills.

Coaches can also reinforce the importance of "thinking hockey" by consistently praising plays that may not make any highlight reel, but do show a player making a smart decision during a play. If we simply respond to goals and assists, our players quickly begin to believe that scoring and winning, not learning, is the main reason to play the game.

The 1983 Edmonton Oilers were an amazingly skilled team. Players like Wayne Gretzky, Mark Messier, Grant Fuhr, and Glenn Anderson led this flamboyant and entertaining squad. It was often stated about this team that they would rather win a game 13 to 12 than 1 to 0. For a defenseman like myself, that attitude did not make my job easy. To a man, however, each player realized that, once the playoffs began, winning took on a whole new perspective. We had to become a tight unit that was solid in all three zones of the ice.

During the playoffs in 1983, we played the Stanley Cup champion New York Islanders in the finals. With their experience, leadership, and tenacity, the Islanders disposed of us in four straight games. I will never forget looking in the mirror of the visitors' dressing room in Long Island as I cut off my playoff beard and wondering how we could possibly beat such an awesome team. As I looked around I noticed similar looks on the faces of many teammates. We were a talented team but never one that was disciplined defensively in our own end, nor in many cases did we listen to the technical suggestions that our assistant coach John Muckler had for us. At the beginning of the next season the transformation of the team was incredible. The players had become focused on accepting any ideas that the coaching staff suggested, anything that might give us an advantage over the year before. It was astonishing to see this group of talented players with such an interest in learning new hockey concepts. It was a tribute to our open attitude to learning that we beat that same New York Islanders team in five games to win the 1984 Stanley Cup!

A Final Word about Mental Preparation

Season after season players across the country practice their technical skills to progress one step closer to their ultimate hockey dream, whether it is a college scholarship, junior hockey experience, professional career, or simply a chance to keep playing the game they love. Older players may realize that physical conditioning for hockey gives them an advantage on the ice that may bring the dream of a professional career dream even closer to reality. For most players, though, it is the mental skills acquired early and throughout their minor hockey years that will make the difference between becoming a good hockey player and truly reaching their ultimate potential!

Appendix

sample practice plans, blank templates
of practice plans, preparation routines,
Emergency Action Plan,
Concussion Guidelines

Appendix

This Appendix contains the following:

1. **Two Sample Hockey Practice Plans**
2. **One Blank Practice Plan Template**
3. **One Sample Dryland Training Practice Plan**
4. **One Blank Dryland Training Practice Template**
5. **Sample Pregame Preparation Schedules**
6. **Sample On-ice and Off-ice Stretching Programs**
7. **Emergency Action Plan—condensed version (from Chapter 7)**
8. **Concussion—Symptoms & Recovery and Guidelines for Return to Play (from Chapter 7)**

These items are intended to be a handy reference for coaches. Permission is given for the charts and plans in this section to be reproduced or adapted for personal use. Being prepared for on-ice practices, for dryland practices, and especially for on-ice emergencies is an important responsibility for every hockey coach.

Hockey Practice Plan I

DATE: _____ **TIME:** _____ **LOCATION:** _____

MAIN PRACTICE OBJECTIVE: <u>Skating</u>

Drill Name	From	To	Key Points
1. Double Circle Warmup	0	5	stretch/agility/ warmup
2. 5-Circle Skating— Elbows on Knees	5	10	bent knees/ good leg thrust
G—Mirror Drill			quick reactions
3. Shadow Drill	10	15	agility/fun
G—Up and Down Drill			up and down skills
4. Attack the Triangle	15	20	stickhandling
G—Spin and Catch Drill			agility/glove speed
5. 4 Corner Circle Pail Drill	20	30	speed
G—T-Drill			positional awareness
6. Full Ice Horseshoe Drill	30	45	1 on 0, 2 on 0, 3 on 0
7. D to W to C Pass & Shoot	45	55	positional play
8. Shootout	55	58	fun
9. Cooldown/Closing	58	60	positive feedback

Permission to Reproduce

Hockey Practice Plan II

DATE: _____ **TIME:** _____ **LOCATION:** _____

MAIN PRACTICE OBJECTIVE: <u>Stickhandling</u>

Drill Name	From	To	Key Points
1. Double Circle Warmup	0	5	stretch/agility/ warmup
2. Partner Push/Pull	5	10	bent knees/ good leg thrust
G—5 Cone Drill			skating/agility
3. Pig in the Middle	10	15	passing/fun
G—Long Shot Drill			rebound control
4. Attack the Triangle	15	20	stickhandling
G—Spin and Catch Drill			agility/glove speed
5. 1-on-1 Stationary Keepaway	20	30	power
G—Behind the Net Shoot In			puckhandling
6. 4 Corner Box Passing	30	45	passing/shooting
7. 3-on-3 Quick Change Scrimmage	45	55	endurance/fun
8. Caboose Race	55	58	power/fun
9. Cooldown/Closing	58	60	positive feedback

Permission to Reproduce

Hockey Practice Plan _____

DATE: _____ **TIME:** _____ **LOCATION:** _____

MAIN PRACTICE OBJECTIVE: _____

Drill Name	From	To	Key Points
1.			
2.			
G—			
3.			
G—			
4.			
G—			
5.			
G—			
6.			
7.			
8.			
9.			

Permission to Reproduce

Dryland Training Practice Plan

DATE: _____ **TIME:** _____ **LOCATION:** _____

MAIN PRACTICE OBJECTIVE: <u>Speed</u>

Drill Name	From	To	Key Points
1. Slow Warmup	0	5	low tempo, on soft surface
2. Static Stretching Program	5	15	hold for 20 seconds, no pain
3. ABCs of Running	15	25	technique important, not speed
4. Speed & Strength Circuit	25	40	encourage full intensity
a) Lateral Skater Strides			bent knees, good balance
b) Wall Sits			90° knee bend
c) Half Moon Drill			bent knee, full leg extension
5. Ultimate Football	40	60	improved endurance, fun
6. Torso Workout	60	70	core strength improvement
7. Cooldown Run	70	75	slow tempo
8. Closing	75	80	positive feedback

Dryland Training Practice Plan _____

DATE: _____ **TIME:** _____ **LOCATION:** _____

MAIN PRACTICE OBJECTIVE: _____

Drill Name	From	To	Key Points
1.			
2.			
3.			
4.			
a)			
b)			
c)			
5.			
6.			
7.			
8.			

Pregame Preparations Schedule

MORNING GAME PREPARATION

Game Time	10:00 AM
Pregame Meal Time	8:00 AM
Pregame Meal	Pancakes/Toast/Muffin/Cereal
	Orange/Apple/Grapes
	Juice/Skim Milk
Off-ice Stretch	Begin at 9 AM at home/rink
Complete Dressing	9:45 AM
On-ice Stretch	10:00 AM

AFTERNOON GAME PREPARATION

Game Time	1 PM
Pregame Meal Time	10:00 AM
Pregame Meal	Waffles/Toast/Jam Sandwich
	Orange/Apple/Grapes
	Juice/Skim Milk
Off-ice Stretch	Begin at 12 PM at home/rink
Complete Dressing	12:45 PM
On-ice Stretch	1:00 PM

EARLY EVENING GAME PREPARATION

Game Time	6:00 PM
Pregame Meal Time	2:00 PM
Pregame Meal	Spaghetti/Bread/Salad
	Fruit Salad
	Juice/Skim Milk
Off-ice Stretch	Begin at 5 PM at home/rink
Complete Dressing	5:45 PM
On-ice Stretch	6:00 PM

LATE EVENING GAME PREPARATION

Game Time	9:00 PM
Pregame Meal Time	5:00 PM
Pregame Meal	Spaghetti/Bread/Salad
	Fruit Salad
	Juice/Skim Milk
Off-ice Stretch	Begin at 8:00 PM at home/rink
Complete Dressing	8:45 PM
On-ice Stretch	9:00 PM

PREGAME SNACK OPTIONS

banana, fig bar, glass of juice, granola bar, jam sandwich, crackers, bagel

Pregame Stretching

OFF-ICE STRETCHING PROGRAM

Encourage players to make static stretching part of their prepractice and pregame routine in order to enhance flexibility and to regain valuable ice time lost due to players stretching on the ice.

The following stretches are described more fully in Chapter 5 on pages 128 to 132. Hold all stretches for 10 to 20 seconds.

STRETCH #1—Ankles

Sit upright with one leg crossed over the other. Hold just above the ankle and grasp the toe with the other hand. Slowly rotate the foot.

STRETCH #2—Calf Muscles

Stand upright 2 or 3 steps from a wall. Lean against the wall keeping a straight line of head, neck, spine, pelvis, leg, and ankle. Keep heel of straight leg flat on floor. Bend arms and move chest towards wall.

STRETCH #3—Hamstring Muscles

Sit upright on a bench with one leg extended straight out in front. Keeping leg straight, exhale and bend at waist moving upper body forward. Keep back straight.

STRETCH #4—Groin A

Sit upright with legs flexed and heels touching. Grasp ankles and pull them close to buttocks. Lean forward keeping hips and back straight. Try to lower chest towards the floor.

Permission to Reproduce

STRETCH #5—Groin B

Kneel on all fours with toes pointed backwards. Keeping arms straight, slowly spread knees apart and try to lower hips to floor.

STRETCH #6—Quadriceps/Thigh Muscle

Stand upright with legs together. Bend one knee and hold foot close to the buttock with the same hand. Keep back straight and knee pointed down.

STRETCH #7—Hip Flexor Muscles

Kneel on one knee with other bent at 90° and foot flat on floor. Slowly move hips forward keeping back straight.

STRETCH #8—Abdominal Muscles

Lay face down placing palms on floor beside hips. Slowly press down on floor and raise head and trunk while arching back.

STRETCH #9—Trunk Muscles

Grasp a hockey stick with both hands and rest on shoulders. Turn upper body to one side as far as possible, hold, and then turn to the other side.

STRETCH #10—Shoulder Muscles

Sit upright with arm raised to shoulder height. Flex arm across to opposite shoulder grasping raised elbow. Pull elbow across the chest.

ON-ICE STRETCHING PROGRAM

As a partner to the off-ice static stretching, a dynamic stretching routine at the beginning of each practice will enhance players' flexibility and develop a moving awareness of body position, coordination, and balance. Stretching drills performed while skating are a valuable addition to an otherwise stationary stretching routine performed at home, in the dressing room, or in the lobby of an arena.

DYNAMIC WARMUP DRILL FAVORITE

Double Circle Drill

This is an ideal warmup drill for leading a dynamic stretching routine.

Description

The coach stands just outside the blue line in the mid-ice area. Players skate slowly through the middle of the ice duplicating the stretch that the coach is demonstrating. Once they reach the front of the opposite net, players curl off to either side and skate back up the ice beside the boards using slow but deliberately long strides.

By encouraging players to lengthen their strides, coaches can begin to teach proper balancing and coordination skills as well as initiate one of the important components of becoming a faster skater—increased stride length. (Increased stride frequency is the other.) As the players return down the mid-ice area the coach demonstrates another stretch until all the appropriate body parts have been stretched. As they skate by, every player has a perfect view of the demonstrating coach and they gain a solid understanding of how to perform each stretch.

Here is a selection of dynamic stretching drills that can be performed in the "Double Circle Drill":

Permission to Reproduce

SHOULDER REACH

Players hold their sticks over their heads as far up as possible for a few seconds, then bend over at the hips to touch their sticks on the ice. Repeat 3 or 4 times skating down the ice.

FOREARM ROTATIONS

Players keep their arms extended in front of them and rotate their sticks in a circular fashion, stretching out the forearm muscles. Players use both arms as they skate down the ice.

BACK ROTATIONS

Players hold their sticks behind their backs and turn left and right while standing straight up. As a variation players bend over at the hips. The turning left and right continues down the entire length of the ice.

IN AND OUT

Players skate with both feet on the ice, extending their legs as wide as possible and then bringing them in as close as possible. This "In and Out" maneuver continues down the length of the ice.

FRONT LEG KICK

Players keep their arms and stick extended directly in front of them and attempt to slowly kick one leg up to touch the stick at chest height. The supporting leg must be kept bent while kicking and the movement must be slow and deliberate to avoid injury. The players kick alternating left and right legs as they progress down the ice.

SLALOM COURSE

Players keep their skates on the ice and completely together, similar to a downhill skier. They keep their knees bent and push off inside edges as they progress down the ice.

CROSS OVER

Players advance down the ice, crossing one skate in front of the other continually. Players improve hip flexibility with this movement in preparation of full speed skating and direction changes during practice.

Emergency Action Plan

Three main people are involved in an Emergency Action Plan:

1. Charge Person
2. Call Person
3. Control Person

The duties and responsibilities of these important people are described below.

CHARGE PERSON—INJURY EVALUATION

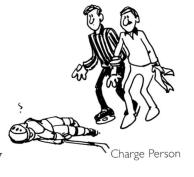
Charge Person

- Safely get to the injured player.
- Determine if the player is conscious by asking a question.
- If loss of consciousness, then initiate **EAP**.
- If the player is conscious, then ask if the player has any neck pain.
- If neck pain, then initiate **EAP**.
- If absolutely no neck pain, then slowly remove player from ice surface.
- Accompany the player to the dressing room for further evaluation of the injury.

CHARGE PERSON—DURING EAP

- Ensure that the player is not moved at all. Immobilize the player's neck by firmly placing hands and forearms on either side of the head without moving it.
- Signal the call person to show that help is required and that a call should be made for an ambulance.

Pre-arranged Signal

- Never allow the player's head, neck, or body to move until experienced ambulance personnel arrive at the scene.
- Monitor the player's breathing if he remains unconscious.
- Accompany the injured player to the hospital and provide pertinent medical information and details of the injury to the hospital medical staff.

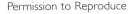

HOCKEY

CALL PERSON—INJURY EVALUATION

- Know the location of a working telephone, the correct emergency telephone number in the area where the arena is located and sufficient change, if required.
- Know the best route to the arena and the most appropriate entrance for the emergency personnel to use, considering ease of stretcher use and ice surface access.
- Report back to the charge person once the emergency call has been made and tell him the estimated time of arrival of the ambulance.

Call Person

- Go to the emergency access area of the arena that will be used and wait for the ambulance.
- Direct the emergency personnel to the proper location in the building.

CONTROL PERSON

- Safely enter the ice surface and approach the site of injury.
- Ensure that any crowd around the injured player is dispersed.
- May then be instructed to relay information to the injured player's parents if one or both are present in the arena.
- Be available for any physical assistance that the emergency personnel may require while transporting the injured player out of the building.

Control Person

Concussions—Symptoms & Recovery

Types of Concussions	Indicators	Recovery Time
First Degree	no loss of consciousness	symptom* free in 15 minutes
Second Degree	no loss of consciousness	symptoms* for longer than 15 minutes
Third Degree	loss of consciousness	

Guidelines for Return to Play**

First Degree Concussion	Return to play after 20 minutes with no symptoms. The Canadian Hockey Association recommends that any player suffering a first degree concussion should be seen by a physician before returning to play. After a second first degree concussion, no play is allowed for one week after all symptoms have cleared both at rest and with activity. After three first degree concussions in one season it is recommended that players discontinue active participation in a contact sport for the remainder of the season.
Second Degree Concussion	Return to play after being symptom-free for one week. After two second degree concussions, return to play after two weeks symptom-free. Discontinue active participation after three second degree concussions in one season.
Third Degree Concussion	Return to play after being symptom free for two full weeks. After two third degree concussions in one season, return to active participation after being symptom free for four weeks. Discontinue active participation after three third degree concussions in one season.

* Post-Concussive Symptoms: dizziness, headache, confusion, blurred vision, nausea, poor concentration, memory changes

**Guidelines of the American Academy of Neurology

LifeSport Books

Watch for others in the LifeSport Books series. The first will include:

Hockey: Drill Solutions

Hockey: Dryland Training

And many more on individual and team sports.

Play games for life!

For more information call:

HENDRIKS
PUBLISHING LTD.

4806–53 St.
Stettler, AB, Canada T0C 2L2
Phone/Fax: 403-742-6483
Toll Free Phone/Fax: 1-888-374-8787
E-mail: editor@fphendriks.com
Website: www.fphendriks.com

COACHING NOTES

COACHING NOTES

COACHING NOTES